SOON AND VERY SOON:
A SPIRITUAL/POLITICAL
PHROPHETIC VIEW:
Second Edition

By Elder Gideon Odinga Mukhtar

[Type text]

Dedication and Acknowledgements

*To my six grandchildren: I
pray they grow to be the living
epistle of ELOHIM
And future generations of righteous
Revolutionaries*

**Nefertiti Kaprice Odinga Pope
Akiem " odinga pope" Burgest
Amon " odinga pope" Burgest
Azikiwe Kamou Odinga Pope
Ndanu Eugenia Odinga Pope
Myjhani Latrice White Odinga
Pope**

Special Acknowledgement
Bishop Melvin Brown
YESHUA Temple of Praise
Philadelphia, Pa.

I thank ELOHIM for the
direction and guidance I
have received from Bishop
Brown. I am indeed
blessed to be a minister of
the YESHUA Temple of

**Praise. Without the help of
Bishop Brown, this work
would not have been
possible! Bishop, turda
and may you go in grace
and the power of the spirit**

**YESHUA Temple of Praise
Philadelphia, PA
bishopmbx@live.com**

About the Author

*Elder Gideon Odinga Mukhtar{
Oliver E. Pope}is a minister of the YESHUA
Temple of Praise, located in Philadelphia,
Pa. He has been an ordained minister for
eleven years. He is also a Revolutionary
Pan-Africanist Minister. He has helped
continue the revolutionary Pan-African
legacy at home{ Africa} and throughout the
Diaspora by way of organizations he has
been a part of especially the All African
People's Revolutionary Party{AAPRP} and
All African People's Revolutionary Party-
Guinea Conakry{AAPRP-GC}of which he is
currently a zealous supporter. He has had
over forty four years of experience in the
Civil Rights, Black Power and Revolutionary Pan-
African movements. Elder Odinga has been an
instructor of the Pan-African Studies Continuing
Education program of Temple University, Philadelphia,*

PA, a columnist for the Black Star Community Newspaper, Philadelphia, PA. He is a prolific researcher and writer and to date has written several other books. Elder Gideon, now resides in Savannah, GA where he continues as a minister, researcher, author and organizer.

Prologue

To GOD be the glory! I am a zealous believer in the word of GOD. YESHUA is Lord! I believe in the promises of GOD and in HIS gifts of discernment and prophecy, gifts that are greatly misunderstood and seldom taught about in much Bible instruction, evangelism and preaching. The ALL MIGHTY will give you an ear to listen to the DIVINE VOICE. "The steps of the righteous are ordered by the LORD." (Psalms 3)   It is our intent to speak to this matter.

The world has always been a complicated place of existence for the children of GOD and for the righteous, those who abhor evil and have a zealous disdain for injustice. We humans fell from grace and the way back to divine truth and the Book of Life is by way of spiritual and material struggle, but we are blessed with the blood of YESHUA and grace. In our ordination preparation Bible study, at the Yeshua Temple of Praise in Philadelphia, Pa., our Bishop, Melvin Brown - our warrior leader - would always stress that good preaching and ministering must necessarily involve good teaching. I learned that with regards to ministerial preparation – even in many formal seminary instructions – the topic of discernment, prophecy and eschatological study is seriously lacking, avoided and misunderstood. The reasons for this, I believe, are due to ignorance – an ignorance that is unconsciously and often times consciously passed on to others in classrooms, in churches and in mislead evangelism and stewardship. Unconscious or conscious, in terms of the effects, this is a sin. It stems from a very old issue within Christianity, the ministry, and is found in many institutions of religious belief and theology. It also stems from the attempt by evil in high places to confuse and mislead. I refer to it as the **Sadducee Pharisee complex** - a devilish issue of pride, self-righteousness, opportunism, reprobation and abomination.

Within Christianity - which by way of divine intent was given to humankind by way of African culture *(Dr. Yusef Ben Jochannan: <u>Africa the Origin of Major Western Religions; Blackman of the Nile; also see YouTube video," The Ancient Israelites of the Bible Were Black and Still Are Today</u>)*. This trend of conscious deception can be traced from the errors and self-righteousness of priest, kings and pharaohs of pre Egyptian dynasties*(Ibid. Jochannan; Thomas Mbiti: <u>African Religions and Philosophy</u>)* to the Pharisees, Sadducees and priest of the time that YESHUA walked, to the devilish aspects of the Kabala and it authors; even to the charlatans of Christianity that sought the justification of the depraved Atlantic slave trade, even up to modern times by way of the manipulation and spiritual debauchery of satanic secret orders that were and are of Lucifer and to the current contradictions of many mega-profit-seeking pastors and hustlers within the church and within Christianity in these last days.

There has been a misguiding elitism within theocracy, theology, ministry, evangelism and Christian belief. This flaw is the concept that the masses are not capable of understanding GOD's gifts in regards to the blessings of the higher realms of spiritual glory, the realms of the seven heavens, the domains of discernment and prophecy. How wrong this foolish notion is. **GOD's gifts are for all who seek HIM!**

Also, our purpose in this writing is to clearly indicate the relationship, indeed the harmony, between genuine Christianity and morally correct, justified and righteous political struggle, and here, I use the term political struggle in its epistemological and etymological sense of **a struggle for power and control of a people's culture and destiny.** *{Psalms 3 and 34:17}* Christianity has always stood for righteousness and - <u>an essential component of righteousness is the insistence on the abhorrence of injustice, oppression, exploitation, political dominance and terror.</u> Isaiah 61:1-5 clearly demands the children - indeed the elect of GOD - to take on the infirmities of the weak and to boldly attack evil in its spiritual and earthly-material manifestations.

The term liberation theology has often been used in reference to seeing the Bible as a guide for liberation and "just" revolutionary struggles. Through GOD's grace we are given liberty and life in abundance; this includes being free and being a freedom fighter for a people's liberation. GOD did not mean for man to oppress and exploit one another, and so the Bible and *GOD's way, truth and light* **must be seen as an instrument, indeed a weapon to combat and defeat oppression of any kind**. Too often the Bible has been used to compliment oppression - *to bless the slave ships in the name of Jesus or to justify wars of aggression, plunder and immoral land seizure under such deceitful rubrics as: one nation under God or manifest destiny or the latest deception of the U.S. foreign policy "invading a country for humanitarian reasons.* A look at the chapters of Judges, First and Second Kings, Psalms, Ruth, and Ester, for example, reveals a story of righteous revolutionaries and freedom fighters who were the elect of GOD, mighty men and women of virtue, humility and valor. They were genuine priest of the high order of Miscelzeldek.

This sterling and sacred quality of liberation gospel is tremendously lacking in the ministry and church leaders of today not only in terms of their ministry but also in their political-economic analysis and understanding of current and past world events and in their efforts or lake of efforts relative to community issues and struggles. Too many professed Christians and those who wear the sacred robes are unaware of the Bible and the Bible's clear liberating call and responsibilities implicit in the righteous call in terms of a conscious understanding of the current oppressive systems that are a pestilence to humanity and those governments that encourage such human disregard for human dignity. Too many - who profess to be holy stewards - are sadly naïve and or supportive of the wrong thing, which really questions their Biblical understanding. One cannot salute GOD and at the same time pledge allegiance to tyranny. This writing speaks to this contradiction in spiritual and political depth, particularly in the sections entitled: **Indicators of the End Times and the Role of the Church in the Last Days.** Some may interpret these sections as too much political/economy and worldly concern. Yet, I caution all not to be so *"holy that we are no more earthly good."* Some think it anathema for ministers to mix political struggles with GOD's word. How wrong and confused they are. No doubt, some would think it not decent and in order that this writing is passionate in terms of exposing the myths regarding the State of Israel and the corrupt and anti-christ aspects of the government and economy of the Unites States and the G-8 capitalist countries.

It is also the intention of this writing to show the relevancy of the Word of GOD by way of the analysis of current world events and also by doing so, we hope to give a more practical understanding of the Bible and make it more appealing and relevant to a youthful generation that is very much aware of the current realities of living in this current spiritually and politically tumultuous and contradictory world.

As the world approaches the year 2016, the explosion of dire predictions and evident atrocities and catastrophes surrounding us constantly portrays a clear omen beginning of Revelations Tribulations*{Rev. 3:10}*. It is in pop literature, in the movies, on the news, within international relations, in nature and occurring with a regularity that is beyond alarming and for true believers spiritually sobering. Natural events of unprecedented status are occurring around us, even lighting that has caused fires never seen before and storms that have done damage unimaginable before. Calamity is in every sphere of our lives from suicidal workers to deranged and alienated youth who take to gun play at schools and maniacs roam wild in the streets in a cross section of neighborhoods and ethnic communities. *And "death rides open on the streets and hell right behind it. {Rev. 6}* Seers of illusion and profit have predicted the end of the world down to the exact date; only to be exposed by the reality of another GOD given day. As social relations break down and war wages and ravishes, along with disquieting natural events of unprecedented stature in diverse places; it is no wonder that today many Christians ponder over God's revelation warnings and predictions. Lest we forget, those cautionary revelations also warn us of great deceptions and illusions in the end times and many false prophets. And so again, a genuine understanding of prophecy and how to know genuine prophecy and genuine prophets is essential and included in this writing; moreover, it is imperative to read and know about many world trends and signs of the end times so that the coming great tribulation and great deceptions and delusions will not come on you unaware.

A sincere and rigorous effort has been made to expose spiritual charlatans and great deceivers. In particular, we set out to expose the great deception that is stated below and the myth of a new Jewish people that is associated with it; along with the notion that the United States is a GOD fearing government:

"Fulfillment of end time Bible prophecy was not possible until Israel - the State established in 1948 by imperialist domination and evil interest and intent - once again becomes a nation dwelling in her promised land with Jerusalem as her capitol. The restoration of Jews to their promised land is one of the prophetic signs of the end times. "

Such statements are accepted without question, but the deception in the statement above is as false as the belief that cherubim's are quiet little white rose cheek babies or that Moses and Jesus looked like Charleston Heston. Let us also say that many of the myths, misinterpretations and distortions in the King James Version of the Bible are also dealt with and the deceptions stated above are exposed as an element of imperialistic deception and the rising anti-christ - "All that calls itself Israel is not Israel."{**Romans 9: 6**} Notwithstanding the validity of the King James version of the Bible - in a relative sense - being a good reference source on the word of GOD, the fact of the racist and opportunistic context of its origin and the true reason for its' writing , *"by the Court of King James"* and decisions as to what to include and what not to include in the writing and the lack of acknowledging the African origin of Christianity along with the lack of mentioning the African presence in the Bible, *"by the Court of King James"* makes this writing unique and vital for all Christians and all people, particularly people of African descent!

It is in this regards that in additional to the King James version, it is highly encouraged that other cited sources are referenced in particular the following: The works of Dr. Yuself Ben Jochannan and Dr. Thomas Mbiti sighted above; Dr. John G. Jackson: Introduction to African Civilization; the writings of Dr. John Henrick Clark; knowledge of Hebrew to

English dictionary translations and Hebrew, The Zohar, Dr. John Hope Felder: <u>Black Presence in the Bible</u> and the works referenced throughout this book.

One cannot understand the Bible without the revelation of the HOLY SPIRIT, but one must also realize that correct political consciousness and a good "and truthful" understanding of history is essential – especially Traditional African history.   Political consciousness must also be seen as a gift and - as was stated earlier - is in harmony and consistent with the morality of GOD's word. Fundamental to the understanding of the Bible is a good understanding and background of Traditional African history that is African history before the Hyksos Invasion (1720-1710) BCE

Much Biblical historical record is hidden and contained in the history of African people - *the Hebrews of the time of Abraham, Isaac and Jacob were Africans* - and much has been camouflaged and destroyed because it exposed the hypocrisy and lies of the early church in Europe and the rising greed of emerging capitalism. To this day the lie continues, ***but the WAY, the TRUTH and the LIGHT will expose the darkness!***

We also seek to show how you can escape the great trial and great tribulation that is coming on this prophetic generation by developing a proper understanding of GOD's word and by developing a personal relationship with **YESHUA the CHRIST! The KING of KINGS and LORD of LORDS!**

When the opportunity came my way to write this I said, "YES LORD!" I claim no special calling or anointing. We all have an anointing assigned to us. **We all are called for God's glory; notwithstanding, few - *for the choices we make in this earthly existence* - very few are chosen and given the keys to the kingdom.** Yet, all have an opportunity to receive the keys. GOD's grace is available to all who choose to receive. But, it is we who lock GOD out; however, as long as there is life there has been given grace and mercy. They are new every morning!

Through the dispensations of the MOST HIGH, we have been given grace. In this current *"Six dispensation"*, we have been given exceptional grace, and with this comes the HOLY SPIRIT of understanding, knowledge, foreknowledge and divine wisdom. GOD has repeatedly said that HE would not have HIS righteous ignorant. GOD will let us know the secrets of heaven, *even before they occur on earth*! And remember, it is a gift of grace available to us all! The reason that GOD would not have us ignorant is to protect and save us from spirits of evil, ignorance, fear, hatred, lack of confidence and oppression - spiritual and earthly! GOD does not want us to wreck and so a prophetic view is a map, a GPS to find freedom from oppression and to have: peace, joy and eternal glory. The GPS to glory is contained in a **"WISE UNDERSTANDING"** of the

Basic Instruction Book for Living on Earth!

Take heed to the love, advice and warning of this writing!

*"BEHOLD, THE FORMER
THINGS ARE COME TO PASS,
AND NEW THINGS DO I
DECLARE: BEFORE THEY
SPRING FORTH, I TELL YOU OF
THEM."*

Isaiah 42:9

TABLE OF CONTENTS

SOON AND VERY SOON

CHAPTER ONE

PROPHECY AND IT'S SPIRITUAL AND PRACTICAL SIGNIFICANCE

> *" And it shall come to past in the last days, saith GOD , I will pour out my spirit upon all flesh: and your sons and daughters shall prophecy "*
>
> **Joel 2: 28**

> *" The steps of the righteous are ordered by the LORD "*
>
> **Psalms 3**

Staying in tune and in behavioral sink with GOD's word will not only guide us in our daily pursuits of earthly needs and desires; more importantly, it will insure our return to the Book of Life. Staying in spiritual sink with the eternal living WORD will allow us to hear the voice of the eternal spirit of truth and knowledge - the *HOLY COMFORTOR*. And this voice is one of prophetic announcements and revelations. Our supreme SAVIOR would not have us ignorant. Grace to hear the prophetic voice is available to all to some degree; we all can ascend to the first heaven; furthermore, <u>for GOD's glory and purpose</u>, some have been given a higher anointing - the keys to enter the HOLY OF HOLIES and receive the **SHEKHINAH** blessing. Such was the case for the major and minor prophets. And even to this day, there are some that will receive even greater works. **{John 14:12 }**

Prophecy has practical significance with regards to the daily struggles and experiences of life. What many fail to realize are the daily prophetic guiding GOD gives us. Often times we pass it off as common sense, vibrations, inclinations and "our first thoughts. " *Did you ever realize that your first thoughts are often times GOD's admonitions, warnings and inspirations?* What may seem to be a commonsense inclination or an apparent whimsical vibration could be angels - *"unawares" {Hebrews* **13:2}** sent to protect us, least we dash our toe. **{Psalms 91:11-12}** Many of these experiences are prophetic exchanges between you and your maker. **YAHOVA JARI** has opened up the windows of glory and poured you out a prophetic blessing to guide your daily situation - *nothing really happens by accident!* Often times we just don't know how blessed we are! When considering or deciphering prophecy and prophetic related issues, some prior considerations are in order.

The Beginnings of Prophetic Revelation

Prophecy is based on GOD's WORD as given us through HIS prophets revealed through the SPIRIT of GOD. Sometimes through dreams, sometimes through visions, sometimes through messengers, sometimes through natural and supernatural events and wonders, at times by way of ordinary or extraordinary experiences. GOD can use the prolific variety of HIS creation to give or show us a prophet sign. <u>Understanding and interpreting the message is where we must pray and have faith.</u> The leading problem in the interpretation of prophecy is whether the sign, message or scripture should be interpreted in its actual/natural or literal sense. It is also important to understand the interpretation of prophecy and its divine intended time of action; also, every prophecy is related to other prophecies like the piece of a tapestry to the whole. One must take into consideration the whole matter!

Prophecy, like the Bible, was and is intended to communicate truth about GOD and the universal all, to reveal and show the force of the **LORD GOD OF HOST**, to reveal ethical principles, to provide guidance in human struggle, to reveal moral and material values, to help people, cultures and nations change their spiritual, and material being, to make people so sensitive to the world around them that they actively engage in changing that world for the better, and to encourage people to have compassion for their neighbor and to provide prediction of future events. Prophecy should never be interpreted in isolation from GOD's WORD and prayers for confirmation.
{Num.23:19}
Many prophecies of scripture were fulfilled shortly after their

revelation. At least half of the prophecies of the Bible have already been fulfilled literally. Such fulfillment confirms the fact that unfulfilled prophecy will also be literally fulfilled as one could anticipate from fulfillment already achieved. Fulfilled prophecy is an important guide in interpreting prophecy unfulfilled and generally confirms the concept of literal interpretation of a prophecy.

Prophecies may be conditional or unconditional. This becomes an important part in the conclusion that may be reached from the revelation of the prophecy. If a prophecy is conditional, it is possible it will never be fulfilled. If it is unconditional, then it is certain to be fulfilled, regardless of the human response. This is an area of confusion in the interpretation of prophecy, as some have assumed that prophecy is conditional when there is no supporting data that indicates this.

Practical Application

GOD works in our everyday life and those who are spiritually conscious are blessed even more; GOD rewards those who are aware of his presence. ***Acknowledging the existence of GOD is a form of praising GOD***; and when praises go up blessings come down. The practicality of prophecy occurs in our everyday experiences and problem solving. Consider this, all the New Testament writers testify to the fact that the study of prophecy will motivate holy living. **What could be more practical than that?** When you try to do the right thing, all will work for the good of the LORD, even if it may appear not to, by human standards. Like Shadrach, Meshach and Abednego, we should always stand for what we know is right. GOD is greater than any punishment that could come upon us. Whether GOD chooses to deliver us or not, HE is always worthy of our trust. GOD knows what is best, and HE honors those who trust and obey HIM and gives prophetic guidance to them. GOD has a plan, and HIS plan is down to the intricate detail. GOD knows and is in control of the future. Everything that GOD has predicted has come true exactly as HE predicted. ***Therefore, we should believe and trust that the things HE has predicted for the future will one day occur exactly as GOD has declared.*** Our LORD has said in HIS word that HE is right at our front door, and if we would only open up our hearts and spirit to GOD, HE would come in and have dinner with us. If we would only be spiritually attentive to HIS message, we would hear. If we would only stand still through the turmoil's, questions and complexities of this earthly existence, we would hear

YESHUA's VOICE. GOD speaks to us all the time! We - through our choices - block out the divine inspiration by focusing on the boon box of earthly noise. We oftentimes would rather hear junk noise rather than the symphony of GOD's heavenly orchestra. And why is this? We can only truthfully say, the devil made me do it!

GOD SPEAKS TO US ALL THE TIME!

GOD is a multi-linguist, and HIS versatility and use of mediums to communicate the message is boundless. Psalms informs us that the LORD is in the ear of the righteous. **{Psalms 116:5}** As a child, raised by GOD fearing Christian parents, I would often times pray, and afterwards, I would wait quite anxiously to see if I could hear GOD speak to me. Being a child, I was

single minded on the focus of my
attention and was only expecting to
hear an audible response from
YAWEE.   I was aware of the
experience that the young Samuel had
when he responded to Eli; he heard
GOD call out to him.   As I matured
spiritually, I learned that GOD often
times does not speak to us in an
audible voice. ***GOD is a super-multi-
linguist; HE can speak in a
multiplicity of ways***. To the prophet
Samuel GOD's voice was audible.   To
Gideon , GOD spoke by way of an
angel and fire. To Elijah , GOD spoke
by way of a fiery chariot. To Pharaoh ,
GOD spoke by way of plagues and the
death angel.   To David, GOD spoke
by way of victory in battle. To
Belshazzar the king, GOD spoke by
handwriting on the wall. GOD spoke
by way of a jack ass to Balaam. GOD
is more reliable than the postal service.
HIS message will always get through,
and HIS word will never return void!

GOD can speak to you by way of jazz, Reggie, rhythm and blues, the internet, your mate, your best friend, your child, your pet and by many signs and wonders - *ot maphot*. ***But now , I must give a word of caution***! The devil can also speak by way of all that was mentioned above - with the exception of ot- mophet (Hebrew for the marvelous signs and wonders by which GOD works miracles.) The word of GOD says "my sheep know my voice and will listen to no other." **{1John 10:27 }** So it is extremely important to know the origin of the voice/message you hear. Hearing GOD's voice clearly, <u>in other words to get an undisturbed and clear reception</u> , you must be a consistent reader and implementer of ***HIS WORD! THIS WILL INSURE LITTLE OR NO INTERFERENCE FROM EARTHLY OR DEVILISH STATIC!***

Another practical and even political aspect of prophecy is **"divine insight"** and this is a great repository of moral teaching. And those moral principles are still relevant today. **{Amos 5:24}** which speaks to the spiritual imperative of all genuine believers to seek justice always and to be a righteous warrior combating political and economic oppression, moral degradation and spiritual evil or **{Isaiah 58:3-9}** which speaks to the LORD GOD OF HOST commentate aid of those who are revolutionaries for the righteous of the ALL MIGHTY! *Even ones political consciousness is a blessing. The Bible encourages us to not only pray but to also WATCH - in other words be observant and aware of the world around us; consequently, unconsciousness and political backwardness is a sin!* And this takes us more into the profound spiritual aspects of prophecy.

Profound Spiritual Aspects of Prophecy

Prophecy constitutes almost one-third of the Bible. If prophecy is properly taught, there is no reason for it to divert anyone's attention away from YESHUA. **In fact, it should serve to emphasize the centrality of *THE LAMB OF GOD,* throughout the Bible and all existence and all worlds - known and unknown!**

Fulfilled prophecy is one of the best evidences I know of that the Bible is the inspired Word of God. The Bible contains hundreds of fulfilled secular prophecies pertaining to cities, nations, empires, and individuals. Jeremiah predicted the Babylonian captivity would last 70 years. **{Jeremiah 25:11-12}** Isaiah stated that the children of Israel would be sent home from Babylon by a man named Cyrus. {**Isaiah 44:28; Ezra 1:1**} Daniel predicated the precise order of four great Gentile empires. {**Daniel 2 and 7**} The destruction of Babylon old and new was foretold by a number of the Hebrew prophets. {**Isaiah 13**} The Bible contains more than 300 prophecies about the first coming of Jesus, all of which were literal.

With faith and trust we only need wait on the LORD and our faith and strength will be renewed. Prophetic knowledge encourages patient waiting {**James 5:7- 8**}; provokes earnest watching, {**Matthew 24:36, 42**}, inspires dedicated work {**2 Timothy 4:7-8**}, and enhances our hope. {**Titus 2:11-14**} and Romans{**13:12-13**}. Likewise, Peter calls us to gird up our minds and be sober and holy as we look forward to the revelation of Jesus. {**1 Peter 1:13-15**} GOD's Prophetic Word is a staple for our spiritual growth. We need to taste of HIM daily and thrive on HIS grace. We need to open HIS word up with every sunrise and feast upon it, and we need to do so with believing hearts. The book of Revelation promises blessings to those who read it (or hear it read) and who obey it. **{Revelation 1:3}** it is the only book of the Bible to promise such a specific blessing, but all GOD's Word is designed to bless us spiritually **{Psalm 119},** and that includes the Prophetic Word.

" Blessed is he that readeath, and they that hear the words of this prophecy, and keep those things which are written there: for the time is at hand."
Revelation 1:3

CHAPTER TWO

WHAT THE PROPHETS SAW
"The Four Prophetic Periods"
FIVE REQUIREMENTS FOR GENUINE PROPHECY
THE SEVEN INSPIRATIONS THE PROPHETS SAW

WHAT THE PROPHETS SAW

THE BIRTH OF EL SHADDA- CHRIST

Num. 24:17 - The star that they saw {The star of Jacob and destroyer of the enemies *El SHADDA*

Isaiah 7:14- A virgin shall conceive Emmanuel

YESHUA; HE came; HE ministered
HE died ; HE ROSE

HE ASCENDED

Acts 1:10- HE ascended as was told

Acts 2:28-29- HE would not have HIS righteous ignorant

Acts 1:4- Coming of the *HOLY COMFORTER*;

HE left and comfort came as was told

LOOKING BACK *ON HIS MINISTRY*
HE IS WRITTEN OF THROUGHOUT
THE ***VOLUM OF THE BOOK***
1Corth. 11-26

LOOKING FORWARD TO JUDGEMENT
SALVATION AND THE ANCIENT OF
AGE
Rev 22:16 and Daniel 7:19-27 & 8:23-25
Malachi 4:6 ~ Zachariah 14:4 ~ Acts 1:9-12
~ Daniel 7:13-14 ~ Isaiah 2:1-3 ~ Mica 4:1-
2

CONSIDER THE WHOLE MATTER!
Ezekiel 40:1-38 ~ 2 Peter 3: 7-13

THE END ~ JUDGEMENT ~
SALVATION
Rev 21:2; 21:24; 21:1 Isaiah 65:17&66

THE FOUR PROPHETIC PERIODS

1.**PATRIARCHAL**—B.C. 1921—1491

2. **MOSAIC**—B.C. 1491—1370

3. **JEWISH**—Post Exilic—B.C. 500-400
Exilic—B.C. 600-500
Pre Exilic—B.C. 900-600

4. **APOSTOLIC**—A.D. 27—100

<u>These Prophecies divide themselves into three grand divisions:</u>

1. **PAST** Fulfilled Prophecy.

2. **PRESENT** Fulfilling Prophecy.
; These are the prophecies that refer to the Jews, the Nations, and the moral and religious character of the times.

3. **FUTURE** Unfulfilled Prophecy.

FIVE REQUIREMENTS FOR GENUINE PROPHECY

1. **It must have been made known PRIOR to its fulfillment.**

GOD is all knowing! GOD is omnipresent! GOD is beyond man's

understanding. It is through GOD's grace and purpose that we know what we have need of. The HOLY SPIRIT is the spirit of truth. It is at the gate of **Shekhinah glory** that we enter the realm of prophetic vision. It is only by way of spirit that *we can know before it manifests*. According to the book of Zohar and Psalms, the realms of spirit are like gates, doors, or elevators, each opening up a higher realm of grace, another level of heaven. "Lift up your heads oh ye gates, and be lifted up, ye everlasting doors, and the king of glory shall come in. **{Psalms 24:7}** *(Daniel C. Matt, Zohar Annotated & Explained. p. 29)* SHEKHINAH glory is the beginning gate to all higher spiritual levels. This is the first opening to the powers of the Kingdom. "Through this opening all other supernal openings come into view." *(Ibid; Daniel C. Matt)* When one is in rebellion to GOD, the gate is closed. But, in submission to GOD the gate is opened and, "The inhabitants of the world will discover precious, supernal wisdom previously unknown to them." *(Ibid; Daniel C. Matt),* including the fivefold gift of supernatural divine discernment. **{Isaiah 11:4}** When Joseph had his dream, he crossed the gate of SHEKHINAH glory.

Prophecy lies in the realm of the second heavens. It can reach SHEKHINAH glory. "For now we see through a glass darkly, but then face to face."**{1Corinth.13:12}** The Zohar states that the angel Gabriel is over prophecy - for the will of GOD. ***The spirit realm contains good and evil. One must be spiritually careful.*** The spirit realm must not be entered into frivolously, played with or entered into without the protection of the sacred **BLOOD of YESHUA!** To do so is to court doom. Demonic forces can lurk in this realm. The Biblical proof of this can be understood in contemplating the tragic experience

that was dealt the witches of Endore.
{I Samuel Chapter 28}

"The vision and understanding of the prophet and prophecy are a receptive decorative *WORD FROM THE LORD* by way of the *HOLY SPIRIT* to the human entity or instrument." In the Old Testament the word for prophet is the Hebrew word *ro'eh or hozeh* which translated means seer {someone who can predict the future, a psychic, clairvoyant, oracle and/or fortune-teller.} The witches of Endor were seers. <u>But there is a categorical difference in a seer and a prophet</u>. The seer may have supernatural powers given by GOD - and misused - or given even by the devil that will use this to capture the person at his will! The Hebrew word mavi' is the word that distinguishes seer from prophet. Mavi' translated means one that has been given a *word-*

vision from GOD by way of the HOLY SPIRIT.

While formulating this section, my spiritual leader Bishop Melvin Brown, and I had an interesting and quite humorous conversation. *We discussed how the seer { ro'eh } could not see as far as the { mavi' } prophet.* The devil can never have the vision of GOD. Even though the seer may have a gift to see, they have not been **HOLY GHOST authorized** to speak what they see, or understand what they see. But by *mavi'* there is liberty to speak, interpret, and ***will into reality*** - by GOD - into material manifestation. As Bishop Brown put it, **"This miracle gives some understanding to the saying many are called but few are chosen. One may be called to see but only the chosen can understand and speak it into existence."** One must have the authorization of *YAHOVA TESBAUW - THE LORD*

GOD OF HOST. This is what distinguishes the genuine prophet and the genuine minister from the charlatans and the reprobating frauds and devils that lurk in the pulpit. For example, there are many people who drive without a license; they have unauthorized power but only for a season. They are fools behind the wheel. The same is true in prophecy and the ministry. Some have no spiritual authorization; just fools behind the vision, fools behind pulpit, but judgment will start at the altar.

2.IT MUST BE BEYOUND ALL HUMAN FORSEIGHT

Essentially, it is by grace and grace alone that the human species is able to accomplish such amazing miles stones in science, literature, the arts and all the triumphs of human culture. Even if there are those millions who never stop to put GOD first or acknowledge and show appreciation for the gifts of life. But the wisdom of man will never pass the power of EL LOHIM! Consequently, prophecy can never be foreseen by humans; for that reason genuine prophecy must not be traced in any way to human foresight. It must be categorically clear that no one could have known.

3. IT MUST GIVE DETAILS

Ambiguity, sweeping statements, nebulousness, are not characteristics of genuine prophecy. Prophecy gives details that are shockingly on the mark and are quantitatively, identifiably and astonishingly specific.

4. A SUFFICIENT TIME MUST ELAPSE BETWEEN ITS PUBLICATION AND FULFILMENT TO EXCLUDE THE PROPHET FROM FULFILLING IT

5. THERE MUST BE A CLEAR AND EVIDENT FULFILLMENT OF THE PROPHECY

"For now we see through a glass darkly, but then face to face."

1Corinth.13:12

The HOLY SPIRIT is the spirit of truth. It is at the gate of Shekhinah glory that we enter the realm of prophetic vision. It is only by way of spirit that we can know before it manifests!

CHAPTER THREE

INDICATORS OF THE APPROACHING ENDTIMES

"The wages of sin is death. "
"If we confess our sins, HE is faithful and just to forgive us our sins, and to cleanse us from all unrighteousness"
1 John 1:9

A righteous minister of GOD, El Hagg Malike El Shabazz -Malcolm X, said once that he could not respect a man that did not have a watch; he placed emphasis and integrity on ones awareness of the time. The same is true with regards to the spiritual time we are currently in - least the bridegroom come and we have no oil in our lamps! I do not claim to have an extraordinary insight into the future but allow me to offer this humble statement regarding spiritual time - a prophetic outlook. *We are at the beginning of the opening of the six seal of chapter Six of Revelations, the beginnings of the birth pains of the genesis of the end times*. The current reality of the world, which is "The Six Dispensation - the spiritual era of Grace

- is approaching its climax and with this, the world approaches the Rapture and the start of the Tribulations. The indicators and forewarnings are clear; the trumpet sound is already approaching our ears or better, the ears of those who can hear! There is no doubt that many will miss the rapture; they will be too captivated in the world to hear, too riveted into the nonsense to hear the trumpet; ***they will have waited too late to get straight!***

CONSIDER REVELATION SIX

Verse 1-2: The angel represented by a beast, (a good angel} has opened the first seal which represents the opening into the future. In chapter five of revelation it is explained that the one who controls the seals is *YESHUA - EL -SHADDA*, the *All Powerful LAMB of GOD*.

Verse 3: Speaks about the rider of the second horse that comes with the opening of the second seal. And he was given great power to take peace from the earth and to kill. This is Lucifer

Verse 5-6: The opening of the third seal concerns the rider of the black horse. This has been misinterpreted by many, as a great deal of Revelations has. Because it makes reference to a measuring scale and commodities, many say this represents capitalism and symbolizes the leading capitalist and western G-8 power- the United States. They also relate this to the beast mentioned in Daniel and Rev. 10, ***but they are confused!*** The Book of Revelations is very specific and - after careful understanding - very clear on the description of United States capitalism and the G-8 imperialistic countries. The United States will take the lead in the building of the fourth beast mentioned in Rev.20, and the evil force that will usher in the anti-christ; but, we will get to this shortly. **The rider of the black horse is an angel (good angel}** that records all actions and will be a witness at judgment to our deeds of good and not good.

  Verse 7-8 Speaks of the pale horse, and upon it rode the evil spirit of death and demons, and torment and the fury of hell followed behind it. This very accurately describes the debauchery, murder, rape, pillage, cruelty, genocidal wars and wars of ignominious conquest, homosexuality, and spiritual wickedness that , like a roaring lion is devouring many in this ending time world.

47

This verse also indicates that death and the devil are different spirits. If you follow the order from verse three to verse 7, you see that the evil spirit of death comes first{falling to sin, wages of death, then hell}.

Verse 9, 10, and 11 speaks of the fifth seal and those who were martyrs for the faith, those who as {Matt. 5: 10-11} speaks of those who suffered for righteousness sake. They cry out and say," How Long Lord." And the time to punish the unjust - **soon and very soon!**

Verse 12-17 : speaks to the ending of Chapter six and it speaks of the six seal. This is crucial ,for we have already seen this and we are to see much more strange sights in the heavens and on earth: cataclysmic and extraordinary natural events , earthquakes, meteoroids hitting the earth, strange sights in the sky, the hearts of men waxing cold, technology used for evil and humans finally realizing that GOD is real.

Hermeneutics is the science of Bible interpretation. Anyone that studies the Bible for the purpose of learning the truth of God's word, must have a method of interpretation that is consistent through the entire Bible. I

48

fear that a large majority of people use the method of interpretation that will make scriptures fit what they already believe, or what they have read or heard from someone else who has been misinformed. This type of interpretation will not lead to the truth. Many times people that have not based their eschatology on sound Bible interpretation will often make false accusations against others and use their self-righteous view for profit, power and status. The Atlantic slave trade is a clear indication of that. The end of the world prediction of May28, 2011, by a false prophet, was a clear example. But an accurate and consistent look at the environmental, geological, political, economic, socio-psychological issues and trends of this time period, along with the realities taken place in this galaxy, are confirming to revelation predictions. **And now, with a good orientation into prophecy, finally, we can go into specifics in our world today.**

The Bible says that one of the ways we will know that the end is near is a dramatic increase in the number and intensity of earthquakes, cataclysmic volcanoes eruptions, natural disasters,

numerous wars, incomprehensible murder,
pillage and killing, and manmade disasters
that are off the charts and astonishingly
unprecedented; we have seen; Tsunamis in
Indonesia, earthquakes in Haiti and the east
coast U.S. , volcanic mud slides in Chile,
droughts in Africa in Asia, unprecedented
storms in Europe and the U.S. We have seen
– even in the U.S. food crisis, insect
infestations that are comparable to plagues,
fires that are unprecedented in terms of
ferocity. We have seen, strange diseases
and shocking pestilence and the catastrophic
effects of a growing global warming. We
have seen an oil spill in the Gulf of Mexico
which threatens to be the greatest ecological
disasters up to this time - even greater ones
are on the way! Marine habitat is being
decimated; fish and birds are dying by the
millions. Recent studies predict that so
much oil has gushed unchecked from the
ocean floor that the spill will travel along the
Gulf Stream currents to foul the beaches of
Ireland, England and France. In addition,
we have seen nuclear disasters in Russia and
Japan – Just wait until the U.S. experiences
its' nuclear disaster. You say when? **Soon
and very soon!** We have seen the slaughter
of the innocent, even while they worship in

church We have seen Black men shot down like dogs by those who are supposed to serve and protect. We are well into the end times!

We have seen the avalanche of ethical and moral desolation among our youth: callous disrespect for GOD, elders, parents, the church and for each other; the concern for human life is worse than the entertainment media and cinema's - profit seeking portrayal of violence. Young females are falling to the ruthless and insidious claws of the demons of lesbianism and the young men to the sodomy debauchery of homosexuality. Same sex marriage – an abomination to GOD – {See Romans 1: 18-32.} The dignities, cultures and lives of millions are at the mercy of the beasts of imperialistic greed and as Minister, Dr. Martin Luther King Jr. sadly pointed out referring to the U.S., **"My own country is the greatest purveyor of violence."** People are vacant from church and millions of young people are biblically ignorant and know nothing of GOD; while much of the ministry and the church are clamoring for riches, prosperity, silver and gold and the material and misleading riches of a demonic masonic quest to be accepted by evil systems and to worship Lucifer.

In today's world men's hearts wax cold. All these are just a few of the clear ending time signs. The Bible has much prophetic advice and warnings regarding the so-called natural and manmade signs that precede the destructive end of time. Most are in the Book of Revelation in detail. In Revelation 6-16 there are three cycles of destruction that are outlined. The cycles are grouped in sevens: seven seals, seven trumpets and seven bowls of wrath. Some interpret the cycles as occurring one after the other in linear time-line fashion. Others view them as occurring simultaneously. The contents of each cycle item are the wrath of GOD being manifested on earth. It even speaks of these current times when the leading world powers of greed are in dire political and economic straights and on the verge of nuclear war and the current realities of strange phenomena on earth and in this galaxy. **The Book of Revelation is divided into three parts:** 1) "the things which thou hast seen" – events of chapter 1. ; 2) "the things which are" – the seven churches that existed at that time and to which John wrote in chapters 2 and 3 ;) "The things which shall be hereafter" – events from chapter 4 until the end of chapter 22.

The Book of Revelation "Apocalypse" is about judgment in the end times. Apocalypse actually means "lifting of the veil" or exposing all to the light of judgment. And why must we be judged? Because humankind fell from grace! In the beginning of - **humans *with souls*** - *we* walked with GOD on earth in the seven heavens (a spiritual happening). But as humans walked in this earthly realm of material - man by choice - has access to both good and evil. In Genesis, this is explained as the situation with the tree, apple and the serpent. Allow me to explain it this way. As caretakers of the planet, GOD gave man much knowledge in this realm that evil also had access to. Remember, satan and a third of the angels were cast down to earth before the creation of humans. We - spirits with bodies - were placed on earth also. Why? Perhaps it was to see how much we loved GOD and would not betray GOD even in the midst of devilish power {allowed) and temptation. I know one thing for sure, I'm so glad GOD loves us more than we loved HIM! Whatever the reason, ultimately - only GOD knows! *HIS ways are above our ways and thinking!*

Humankind had much knowledge but the world {devil} convinced man that more knowledge could be gained. **Man wanted to know good and evil; <u>the question is why in hell would anyone want to know evil</u>**? Man could learn from GOD or from the devil. And the devil enticed man to know war, greed, and to use the earth for selfish means and even *fooled man into thinking he was a god, and humankind " bit " on this and with that fatal bite Adam'(Hebrew for humankind- male and female }; we fell from grace!*

Yet, amazing grace and mercy are new every morning. Sin is the conscious choice of stepping away from GOD; it is only by evil and temptation that satan captures us at his will. **Romans 3:23** is a part of the human earthly experience. It was because of sin that GOD has destroyed the worlds - that is massive and comprehensive annihilation of billions of human life and other life forms. The floods of the times of what is referred to as Noah are an example. According to ancient Zulu legend the world had been destroyed before; in fact their legend holds that this is the sixths world. When compared to the Christian belief of the Sixth Dispensation and current realities of the end times, you have to give profound thought to Zulu legend. The wages of sin is death. By sin, we place ourselves in the need of spiritual rectification and redemption but not without warning, despair, torment, tribulation, destruction and death; and if not corrected and saved then eternal damnation! Just consider the ways we have transgressed. But the signs of the end times are here. The trumpet of the Rapture train is quite audible; the signs of its inevitable and quickly approaching arrival and might are clear for those who have the spiritual eye to see - *the truth, the way and the light.*

HOW WE HAVE TRANGRESSED

Fourteen signs of the approaching Rapture and Tribulation

"And the eyes of them were both opened and they knew that they were naked."

Gen. 3:7

1/ Homosexuality
{ An abomination to GOD, Romans 1: 26-27 }

Matthew 24:37-39 speaks of the vileness of man and the quantum degeneracy prior to the flood. The current reality of the world, particularly in the so-called modern Western societies are enormously more abominable than the time period of Noah, or even of Sodom and Gomorrah. One major sin of Noah's generation was homosexuality; the current tumultuous torrent of homosexual perversion is one of the foretelling signs that show YESHUA is coming to remove HIS church - **soon and very soon!**

On Feb. 4, 2004 (CNN) reported on a story that is a good reflection of the times we are in: "The Massachusetts Supreme Judicial Court has cleared the way for lesbian and gay couples in the state to marry, ruling Tuesday that government attorneys "failed to identify any constitutionally adequate reason" to deny them the right. In a 4-3 ruling, the court gave the Massachusetts state Legislature six months to rewrite the state's marriage laws for the benefit of gay couples." And now in 2015, the U.S. Supreme court has made gay marriage the law of the land of America

Such legalization of debauchery is exactly what YESHUA warned we would be in at the start of the end times. This is a major sign YESHUA is coming very soon. This is the reason why you are seeing all the signs YESHUA warned us about taking place all at once. We have entered into the final days prior to the return of Christ. The Book of Ephesians , Chapter Six, speaks of spiritual wickedness in high places and rulers of darkness in his world. When the Supreme courts can endorse same sex marriage and even the U.S. office of the president can validate such scandalous and anti-christ behavior (Obama's statement made May 5, 2012), then be assured that YESHUA is coming to remove HIS church - **soon and very soon**!

<u>Spiritual and material pitfalls of homosexuality</u>

The most severe judgments in scripture were preceded by homosexual perversions. **The current accelerating pace of moral decline in America** and throughout the world is a self-fulfilling prophecy that the Rapture is soon! The increase of sexual immorality (including promiscuity and adultery in the heterosexual population, the pervasive influence of the gay/lesbian movement in political and media circles- they were powerful enough to influence a U.S. presidential election), the prevalence of lying (perjury), stealing, disrespect for parents, covetousness, and hatred among the nations will accelerate the advent of God's wrath against the world as a whole. God's Law - the standard of morality - is denigrated and/or ignored by most of **Christendom and too many preachers who see the gospel as a means of enjoying the pleasures of the creature instead of them being a true servant of the Creator!** Sex perversion is just a barometer of demonic activity and of the moral state of society. The perverted preponderance of sexual debauchery within the Catholic church and other denominations, the pompous flaunting of such in media and entertainment, the abuse of young children by people in high and influential positions, like the Sandusky incident of Penn State, and the sexual perversions of U.S. secret service and four star generals are clear signposts that the world is well into the end times.

Many credible historians and spiritual leaders have indicated that it was the internal moral fiber of Rome that led to its' demise. When compared with the moral fiber of America today, with its sexual perversions even reaching to so-called higher institutes of learning where predators ambush the innocent bodies of ten year olds, then know the termination of human existence is near. These lusts are generated by unclean spirits (demons) that are infecting the minds of these individuals. Demons that are conjured up by the profit seeking and evil divinization's of a sick media, movie and communication industry and by people who are supposed to be models of uprightness. "The whole head is sick and the heart is faint." {**Isaiah 1:5**} And sexual perversion is just one of a proliferation of sins perpetrated by U.S. capitalism. Such a political economy produces a situation where everyone does what is right in their own eyes and the end result for society is a "dog-eat-dog world" of injustice and chaos.

Sex perversion in society a measure of demonic activity

Those who dwell on unnatural practices – *anti-GOD practices* - are by definition perverted. Those who spend an unnatural amount of time dwelling on natural bodily functions and fleshly desires are therefore perverted. Sex perversion in society is the number one predictor of impending judgment. The most severe judgments in scripture were preceded by homosexual perversion: the flood, the plagues and destruction of Herod's empire, the fall of Jericho, Sodom and Gomorra. These judgments did not come just because of sexual perversion alone. *Sex perversion is just a barometer of demonic activity manifesting in the moral state of society*. Sexual lusting is never satisfied, and it leads to a downward spiral of more deviant activity that is more and more perverse **- sin draws to the lowest depths** .

These unnatural lusts are not generated only by natural human desires. These lusts are generated by unclean spirits (demons) that are infecting the minds of these individuals by way of " the medium is the message" When Hollywood and the record-video industry becomes the standard of ethics and morality for generations of youth and a mainstay for adult leisure and entertainment, and many of the entertainers like JZ and Bounce, Madonna, Nicky Manage, Justin Beaver, Little Wayne, Labran James and an entourage of many more display demonic illuminati and freemason signs and symbols then know, they have been captured at satan's will and;

moreover Lucifer is loose like a roaring beast capturing whomever it can!

EL LOHIM knows when sexual perversion rules in society demons have also enslaved society in many areas. Many spiritual leaders portray satan as a slew footed homosexual. The consequences of this is spiritually and materially tragic. The guiding force for society embraces doctrines of demons where there are no moral absolutes, no LIGHT or any spiritual accountability - a ubiquity of misery and torment. Everyone does what is right in their own self-righteous eyes, and the end result for society is a "dog-eat-dog world" of injustice and chaos. As they say," *the whole dam thing went to hell!* As Don Koenig points out, we must beware of The Body Possessors.

"God created mankind to trust Him and to be containers of HIS Spirit, so that we will be capable to fulfill HIS will for our lives. Instead, many have made themselves containers of unclean spirits. Demons who wish to possess and defile the human race. The type of spirit within a man will manifest itself in outward expressions. Sex perversion is certainly one of those expressions. When the sexually perverse are free to come out of their closets, be aware that other demonic activity will come out of those same closets with them. The intent is to infect society with doctrines of demons and promote warfare against the sons of light. Today we see this doctrine emerging as an increasingly belligerent stand against God's law and against true Christianity."

How much longer do we think GOD will let the madness go on? The geometric increase of homosexuality is a clear indicate that soon and very soon GOD will crush the madness. The Supreme court is not supreme, GOD IS SUPREM. The Supreme court will only make the real Christians become outlaws for JESUS!

2 Timothy 3: 1-9

2/ THE ABANDONMENT OF CARE TAKERS OF THE PLANET

Earth quakes in diverse places
Unusual East Coast quake: Scientists may take months to pinpoint source

By Suzan Clarke and Lyneka Little - ABCNews.com – Tue, Aug 23, 2011 "It takes just about everybody by surprise," he added.

On Monday, the strongest earthquake to strike Colorado in almost 40 years shook awake hundreds of people, toppled groceries off shelves and caused minor damage to homes in the southern part of the state and in northern New Mexico. No injuries were reported as aftershocks continued Tuesday. The New Madrid fault line is best known for some of the most violent earthquakes to ever hit the U.S: a series of four in 1811 and 1812. The quakes were estimated at magnitude 7.5 to 8.0, so strong the Mississippi River reportedly flowed backward. Damage occurred as far away as Washington, D.C., and Charleston, S.C. In another case The 5.8 magnitude quake felt from Georgia north to Canada prompted swift inspections of many structures today, including bridges and nuclear plants. An accurate damage estimate could take weeks, if not longer. And many people will not be covered by insurance. The Bible even describes a great earthquake that will strike Israel, such as never has occurred before. It will be extremely powerful; causing a great rift to open that will run from Jerusalem in both directions all the way to The Mediterranean Sea to the west, and The Dead Sea to the east. The Mount of Olives, east of Jerusalem, will be split in half.

If you read the Word of GOD you will find out that Noah warned his generation that GOD was going to destroy the world with a flood. Noah's generation was involved heavily in homosexuality and many forms of rejection of GOD's word. Looking back at history we now know the people in Noah's generation did not listen to Noah and did not repent of their wicked ways which included homosexuality. For over a hundred years Noah's warning went out but no one except his family listen to him. In the end, GOD made good on HIS warning and the flood came and killed every living things on the planet except those who were in the ark. Geological and historical record shows that during time period of the Noah floods there were massive and cataclysmic devastations; entire continents were devastated and destruction was comprehensive. Entire civilizations disappeared. One geologist and historian gives unquestionable proof of worldwide devastation. Emanuel Valescosky in his work, "Worlds in Collision" is an excellent source on this point.

"And the earth rebelled!"
3/ GOD MADE DESASTERS IN NATURE AND THOSE CUSED BY HUMANS

> *He will bring extraordinary plagues on you and your descendants, severe and lasting plagues, and terrible and chronic sicknesses.*
> *Deuteronomy28:59*
> *The LORD will also inflict you with every sickness and plague not recorded in the book of this law, until you are destroyed.*
> *Deuteronomy 28:61*

In 2011, we saw a record number of tornadoes, extraordinary

flooding, rampant earthquakes, disturbing volcanic eruptions and a tsunami in Japan that none of us will ever forget. In 2012, we have seen an increase in such events, along with bizarre attacks by animals and insects, traumatic droughts and floods, peculiar diseases affecting crops and people, off the charts droughts and harrowing weather changes, unusual astronomic events and a disconcerting barrage of mysterious phenomena. In 2015 we experienced the effects of global warming that produce "dry lightning storms" – thunder along with lightining hitting bone dry areas causing massive fires which killed and destroyed thousands of acres and millions of dollars in property.

So why were there so many natural disasters in 2011,2012 and 2015? Why so much unprecedented phenomena? Top scientists seem to be at a complete loss to explain what is happening. It just seems like there is one disaster or emergency after another. However, in scripture, there are answers. The two passages' from

Deuteronomy offer much insight and explanation. **The further one is away from GOD, the more hell is experienced in their lives, and when governments and nations turn their backs on GOD and even dare to defy GOD, hell shall be the order of the day. {Habakkuk 2: 6-20}.** About 200 years before Jeremiah was born, God's patience with the apostasy of both nations of the divided kingdom, Israel and Judah, began to grow thin and GOD allowed the destruction to take place. Similar to today, The root problem was the degenerate and rebellious condition of every heart.

"My people are fools; they do not know me. They are senseless children; they have no understanding. They are skilled in doing evil; they know not how to do good." (Jer. 4:22)

4/ THE GROWTH OF KNOWLEDGE WOULD EXCELERATE IN THE END DAYS

"Knowledge shall increase and men shall run to and fro."

{Daniel 12:4 }

With the impact of the internet, e-mail, fax, Facebook, twitter and the abundance of computer software, the spread of information is ubiquitous and penetrating, even to the most remote village in the most dense jungle. I was amazed to learn that during the morally legitimate struggle of the people of Somalia against the U.S. invasion, general Adeed ,was intercepting U.S. pentagon codes by hacking on his laptop while in his mountain guerrilla hideout.

Knowledge is readily available *but not necessarily wisdom and understanding.* The words to and fro are mentioned in the passage from Daniel. This implies that knowledge is being used for those things that are not in our best interest; all types of information are in cyber space and in the hands and minds of billions from children who are victims of child pornography to right wing terrorist having access to getting manuals for making a nuclear bomb and even the privacy of many are open to

SOON AND VERY SOON

scrutiny and surveillance by U.S. governmental forces[1]

Knowledge is going to and fro and everywhere but very few good places. Technology in the hands of one person and/or government - *captured by Satan's will -* is an evil designed favoring the interest of lust, greed, and the most ignominious of transgressions from GOD!

The countries of the world with the most advanced technologies, the G-8 capitalist countries, have used this knowledge more for weapons and profits than for wisdom and prudence! Captured by satan's will and consequently guided to the death of man, the G-8 countries have shown themselves to be the harbingers of the period of the anti-christ. The RFID computer chip and related technologies are examples of the manifestations of end times signs.

---

[1] .{ **30 Signs That The United States Of America Is Being Turned Into A Giant Prison**
Every Breath You Take, Every Move You Make –
14 New Ways That The Government Is Watching You{ Massive expansion of domestic spying under Obama By Niall Green 10 July 2012 wsw.com }

Revelations 13 speaks of the mark of the beast.

Revelation speaks of a time when no one can buy or sell without the computer chip mark. Consumer choice and the so-called "market" can now be literally controlled using computer technology that allows for a mark of the beast economic system. More than ninety-five percent of buying and selling in the industrially developed part of the world is now controlled by computers and the Internet. Computer chips have even been developed that can be implanted in the human body to replace credit and debit cards, and perhaps guide thinking; it is said that the devil first enters by way of our thoughts; " as one thinketh." Similar chips have been created to track criminals and pets and military personnel by satellite. RFID Chips - the more advanced identification chips now being developed - will soon be placed within all products sold. There are plans to put up 66 low orbit satellites around 2015. They will cover all of the earth with communications just like all of the earth is now covered by GPS satellites for location. Some think that we are not far from the time when a chip implanted in the hand could establish a direct <u>neural link</u> with the brain. Soon all people who allow the mark of the beast to be implanted may have a full time neural link to huge amounts of information in the world linked through the internet **and they may also have a link from their brain to the Antichrist - mark of the beast - economic system of Revelation**. The phasing in of such technology has already taken place with the mesmerizing effect of the new computer gadgets and toys. In no time people or those who are clueless as to what is taking place - will be convinced to put their bank account on a chip under their skin and if not convinced, then the government will step in by " manifest destiny and national security" and order it so, and the will of satan will prevail. A world authoritarian evil force {the anti-christ} will at some point use this mature computer technology to its' advantage to try to manage the world and the implementation of the polices listed in the book of Revelation (where no one can buy or sell without the mark of the beast) . This will assuredly take place *soon and very soon!*

5/ SATURATION OF THE GOSPEL TO EVERY LANGUAGE, TRIBE AND PEOPLE

"And this gospel of the kingdom will be preached in the whole world as a testimony to all nations, and then the end will come."

{**Matt. 24:14**} & **Mark 13:10**} "And the gospel must first be preached to all nations." & {**Rev. 14:6**} "Then I saw another angel flying in midair, and he had the eternal gospel to proclaim to those who live on the earth *--to every nation, tribe, language and people."* What the devil means for evil GOD can turn to good. Such is the case with the advance in technology. The positive aspect of this is that the gospel is also now available even in the densest jungle. One can even download the entire Bible to a throwaway cell phone. **YESHUA** is not coming back until all have had access to the gospel. Computers technology is making it so that every I is dotted and every T is crossed, and nearly all have at least heard or read the pronouncement that *YESHUA is LORD!*

6/ THE ACCELERATING GROWTH OF SPIRITUALISM AND ITS PERVASIVE TEACHINGS

Growing up in the church, as a youth, I use to think that spirit and spiritualism was always associated with GOD or angels or at least something related to GOD's grace. Careful reading and understanding of the Bible reveals that spirit can refer to GOD and Good or the devil and evil! The Bible tells us that demons do exist, and that they can manifest in material form and they can take over bodies. Man has always symbolized satan by charts, pictures, omelets, trinkets and paintings. In many instances this was done as a sign and method of adoration of Lucifer. A cursory research into the history of the illuminati and the origins of Freemasonry gives ample evidence to this ignoble fact. Here one must be under grace and be careful, for these symbolisms can open up realms that we are not aware of or at least we may not be in the

74

correct spiritual state to travel in these realms. The case of the witches of Endore is an example.{1 Samuel 28:3-25} Yet, Revelations reveals that in the end times these signs of evil will be pervasive and that society will be saturated with them. The movies, record industry, and entertainments of leisure and pleasure are all contaminated with evil symbols - portals to hell! Evil is preparing its overt entrance into the world. And when we see these signs all around us know that the end is *soon and very soon!*

7/ TINKLING SYMBOS, FALSE TEACHERS, and MONEY PREACHING , <u>SATANS IN THE PULPIT: A FORM 0F GODLYNESS – BUT IN ESSENCE, REPROBATION</u>

{2 Peter 2:1-3&Matthew 13:25-30}

When I was studying for my ordination in 2006, Bishop Brown did several seminars and discussions on the topic of "decent and in order." The emphasis was on church protocol and cordialities within the ministry and in relation to church officials. The crux of attention was focused on respect among church officials and proper ways to resolve contradictions. I learn that within the ministry, it is frown on by many for a minister to criticize another minister in public. This is a touchy subject and must be approached with a grain of "light inspired salt!" One could use this to give respectful and principled criticism at the right time; however, one could also use this axiom of church protocol for malicious intentions   and like Eli in the Bible, use it to hide contradictions, self-righteousness and consequently sin! <u>I say all this to preface an acid criticism of the ministry and to expose a contradiction of self-righteousness and reprobation within the ministry and the church and to do it with a Josiah spirit! {2 Kings 21-22}</u> and to be consistent with <u>{Ezekiel 2:3-6}</u> "He said: 'Son of man, I am sending you to the Israelites, to a rebellious nation that has rebelled against me; they and their fathers have been in revolt against me to this very day. The people to whom I am sending you are obstinate and stubborn. Say to them, **"This is what the Sovereign LORD says**." And whether they listen or fail to listen - for they are a rebellious house - they will know that a prophet has been among them." Some things must be said for the good of the ministry and the earthly body of GOD - the church, and as it is divinely advised in **{<u>Ezekiel 2:3-6</u> },** not to tell the truth is disobedience. I am too afraid of GOD not to be obedient.

Ecumenical unity at the price of doctrinal truth leads to perversion of beliefs.

"Worshipping a wrong concept of God is idolatry." A definite end time indicator is the prolific amount of prosperity ministries, mega-profit-making churches, and material motivational speaking preachers who are caustic and egregious in their false teachings and invidious to any semblance of apology. Thy are flooding all channels of mass media. And certainly we cannot leave out the ministers that are the apologist for U.S. imperialism like Pat Roberts and the Billy Gram types, and other right wing puppets of satan. And I certainly cannot leave out the mendacious ministers of forgery among African people; those plantation preachers that will use and distort GOD's word to defend and protect the "current day masa - the racist American capitalist system" These charlatan and opportunist abuse their sacred intended office for their own gain. I speak of all those who seek to bow to the lesser light and hide behind secrecy; those who instead of standing tall like the Hebrew men who would not bow to Belshazzar; cower and cringe behind their pedestals of safety and comfort and willfully genuflect to Baal, and the current day manifestation of evil - American capitalism and morally filthy Zionism! **Ezekiel 8:18** warns " Mine eyes shall not spare; neither will I have pity; and thou they cry in my ears with a loud voice , yet will I not hear them. " Josiah had the right idea when he resolved the contradiction during his day by literally taking off the heads off those perpetrators of the high order and crushing to powder their idolatries and their lifestyles and putting a righteous end to; those who… *crept in while men slept and sowed snares among the wheat {Matt. 13;25}*

"But there were false prophets also among the people, even as there shall be false teachers among you, who privily shall bring in damnable heresies, even denying the Lord that brought them, and bring upon themselves swift destruction."
                    2 Peter 2: 1

8/ PEOPLE WILL FORSAKE THE TEN COMMANDMENTS AS A MORAL CODE, COMMITTING ADULTERY, STEALING, LYING AND KILLING

> *(Matthew 24:12)The institution of marriage would be forsaken by Many*
> *(1 Timothy 4:3)*

Today, we have generations of youth that are Biblically ignorant and morally backward; a generation who's head is sick and who's heart is faint. We see it in the callous mass shootings and senseless killings. We see such abhorrence in movies and videos. We hear of young mothers throwing newborns in trash dumps and children killing parents and grandparents. The standards of conduct are defined not by GOD's word but by vain – system made – rappers like Little Wayne and J-Z. The divorce rate outstrips the rate of those

couples who stay together. Homosexuals define presidential campaigns, schools rush to abandon prayer and the highest court of the land condones abomination. Corporate moguls and CEO steal the public blind and are excused by presidential bail outs , **and death rides high on his horse and hell right behind it.**
"PROFESSING THEMSELVES TO BE WISE; THEY BECAME FOOLS."
Romans 1:22

9/ THE POSSESSION OF JERUSALEM WOULD BE AT THE CENTER OF INTERNATIONAL TURMOIL

SPECIAL FOR EXPLANATION OF THE TRUE AND FALSE ISRAEL

"Behold, the days are coming, declares the LORD, when I will make a new covenant with the House of Israel and the House of Judah

Jeremiah 31:31

" But this is the covenant that I will make with the house of Israel after those days,

declares the LORD: I will put my law within them, and I will write it on their hearts. "

Jeremiah 31:33

NEVER HAS GOD SAVED AN EVIL EMPIRE

What I argue against

All that calls itself Israel is not   Romans 9:6

When considering the above statement, the question is what does one mean by Israel? **If they are referring to the State of Israel that was created in 1948, then they are grossly confused and definitely wrong!**

It has to feel indescribably awesome to know that you are a child of GOD; to know that you are one of GOD's chosen people. You would have to feel that you are special, and that in store for you are miraculous things. And your inheritance -

81

off the hook good, surpassing all understanding! *Well divine serendipity is for you! The gift of divine adoption is available for those who would receive, but only for those who are in truth and would receive the TRUTH*! The Nation State of Israel – **Settler Colonial Israel** – that was set up in 1948 is an abdominal and horrendous living lie!

The word Israel is derived from the ancient Hebrew dialect, specifically Aramaic dialect; a language spoken by the people of the area of Western Asia. Its roots can be traced even to the Ashanti of West Africa who still use the word Hebrew in their vocabulary. The people of this area at the time of Yeshua{Jesus} were indisputably Black people; thick beautiful lips, short strong hair, broad noses and predominantly very dark skin, Africans. There is an excellent video on YouTube entitled, *"The Biblical Israelites were Black and Still Are Today. "* Many from other areas: Asia and Europe referred to them as people with the burnt shin or Ethiopians; in fact Africans of this area and during this time were called variety of names: Sumerians, Canaanites, Philistines,

Moabites, Hebrews, the people of Punt, Chadian[2]

This fact is vital and culturally significant and essential to get a true understanding of the historical context of the Bible - the word of GOD given to the people of this area to be shared with humanity. But, as we know, history { his-story- those Europeans that choose to write racist and a-historical history } can be a licentious self-righteous tale, a tool to demise other cultures and profit on their misery! Because we are Christians - adherents and internalizers of the *" way", the "truth" and the "LIGHT"* - the GOD truth must be told. ***The original Hebrews and people of Israel and Judah were Africans***. This fact also is credence to the fact that YESHUA, the descendent of forty two African generations was also an African. The WORD was made flesh - African - flesh and dwelt amongst us. **The**

---

[2] **.** (See: **Runoko Rashidi : African Presence in Early Asia - GLOBAL AFRICAN PRESENCE Home Page ; Email Address:runoko@yahoo.com- Web: www.cbpm.org/gapwww.travelwithrunoko.com; Also earlier references to Back presence in the Bible listed in Prologue**).

divine mission for YESHUA was to come to save all of humanity regardless of culture or color, for as the Zohar expresses, we are all particles of heavenly stardust emanating from the GOD of everlasting to everlasting! The supreme spiritual principle of this is that GOD THE FATHER is spirit and therefore absence of color or matter, whereas, The WORD, was made material flesh but at the same time not man- for YEASHUA was the only son of man and son of FATHER GOD. HE was born perfect!

We have given just a brief - well substantiated - explanation as to the original demographics of the area of what today many refer to as Israel – *its' justified name is Palestine!* With the invasion and migrations of the people of western Asia, particularly with the Hyksos invasions and other invasions and migrations from further east, the area was to experience a mixing of cultures and with this also conflict. *(Chancellor Williams: The Destruction of Black Civilization)* As Cheikh Anta *Diop* shows in *Ancient African Civilization* and *From Civilization to Barbarism*, the mixing of cultures - particularly the force mixing of cultures, added with diet, and customs, had a dialectical effect on the people , their habits, customs and even bone structure and skin complexion, consequently; we have what some have termed the Arabnization of the area. **I disagree with this categorization**; I think it diminishes the great culture of the people of Western Asia, a culture that in many ways is very similar to African culture. Instead of Arabnization, I will refer to it as the amalgamation of cultures where the distinguishing characteristic between different peoples is not necessarily color but history, in short, culture. *{Sekou Toure: A Dialectical Approach to Culture, Black Scholar Magazine)* Consequently, over centuries the African Philistines became the great Palestinian people of today and the Hebrews of that time came to find themselves on slave ships and oppressed in their own land!

During the time of the Biblical gospel, the dominant culture and people were Africans and the dominant oppressors were White, Romans! But more importantly this is vital in the analysis of the "**truth, even better the lie**" in the statement that the modern State of Israel and world Jewry {and this implies a significant number of Zionist

hiding under the cover of Judaism } are the chosen of GOD, and that GOD will save Israel{ the State }. **No! The State of Israel as well as its' major financial and military backer, the U.S. will go down by the fires of GOD's anger and a new Jerusalem will be built, or earth and in heaven!**
The Great Deceiver: comes in a thousand disguises; it may steak up on you; but don't let it surprise you! Myth can serve to encourage or discourage. Myth can be an inspiration, or it can be a trepidation, and when myth comes to be the justification and the launching pad for onslaughts of land seizure and military annexation of the sovereign rights and dignities of a people, their culture, their land and its' resources, it is then that myth becomes terror, racist and evil spirited! In modern history, such was the tribulation of the peoples of western Asia and Africa.

A European social mass of thousands of poor and exploited, from various parts of Europe: Germany, Poland, Spain, and the Eastern Pales Settlement of Russia were led - in fact super-bamboozled - by an elite of profit crazed, power ravished and spiritually bankrupt empire seekers who after the

notorious Basil Switzerland World Zionist
Congress of 1887, became known as Zionist,
oftentimes very inappropriately called Jews!
{See Lennir Brinner; Zionism in the Age of Dictators}
This force of Zionism, aided primarily by
the imperial powers of France, Britain,
Germany, Spain, Italy, Russia, the United
States and by the apartheid regime of South
Africa, this Zionism - an evil to humanity
and an abomination to GOD - fell like
broken lighting from the sky on western
Asia, Africa and the world.

**AIN'T NO WAY GOD WOULD BLESS
SUCH! GOD'S WORD CAN NEVER
CONTRADICT ITSELF OR RETURN
UNFULFILLED.**

*I offer you three good reasons why GOD
would not and will not save   the
Nation State of Israel*

1/ The Land is the Palestinians

*" The plain fact is that we Jews are not a
race and we should not let the Zionists
persuade us that we are. Proof to the*

SOON AND VERY SOON

*contrary lies in Palestine, plain for all to
see. "*
<u>What Price Israel</u>, by Rabbi 18<u>Alfred M. Lilienthal</u>

" I KNOW YOUR WORKS, AND TRIBULATION AND POVERTY, BUT YOU ARE RICH AND I KNOW THE BLASPHEMY OF THEM WHICH SAY THEY ARE AND ARE NOT, BUT ARE THE SYNAGOGUE OF SATAN."

"JEWS NOT A RACE OR PEOPLE, BUT ADHERENTS OF A Religious BELIEF!"

The three quotes above are a revelation as to the true nature and deception of a great deal of Zionist literature and false ideological justifications. The quotes dispel the myth of "a land without a people for a people without land." Moreover, they show how detrimental the Zionist movement can be to honest-genuine Jews and those who struggle for justice. The quotes also indicates the abyss of difference between Judaism and the political ideology of Zionism! Zionism has often been innocently defined as <u>a movement to provide a homeland and refuge for Jews in need of safety in the land where their ancestors lived in ancient times.</u>" **That definition only sounds good until we realized that almost a million Palestinians Arabs <u>already living there were forcibly displaced and made homeless.</u>** Incredibly, even today so many years later, many Americans and so many others worldwide, still believe that current day Israel was and is the land without a people for a people without land. **It was not***! "Any real chance for Middle east peace - as well as defusing the reason behind our American led - war on terror - must be based on fact and not on intentional or unintentional distortions of past events."* **{*Rabbi Alfred M. Lilienthal;* <u>What Price Israel</u> }**

The original Hebrews were Africans and the historical roots of the Palestinian people is closely aligned with African people. Palestinian people should be considered first cousins to the African, particularly when one considers the close proximity that the two people's live. It is similar to the relationships that exist in those border neighborhoods that comprise Black

SOON AND VERY SOON

and Latino people - for generations! Not only will the complexion change but also the language and aspects of culture; notwithstanding the fact that the dominant culture will always prevail. **The statements that the area of Palestine - which includes the British created state of Jordan in 1921 - is the home of the current citizens of the State of Israel is a myth of European Zionist!**

Malcolm X - another great fighter for justice, liberation and an acid critic of Zionism – said that "of all our studies history is best qualified to reward our research." History shows that the African was the first of the human species. Moreover, truly objective history shows that from Africa the human species spread throughout the world. *{Diop: <u>Ancient African Civilization</u> ; W.E.B. Du Bois: <u>The World and Africa</u>}* The first people to live in the area that we today refer to as Western Asia - {**<u>incorrectly referred to as the Middle East</u>**} were indeed the African. The next great culture to inhabit the area was the Palestinians; and then came the invaders from eastern Europe. *AND THAT IS THE GOD'S TRUTH!*

2/ True Israel & false Israel

Even before the 4th millennium B.C, Palestine was inhabited by herders and farmers. It was in the 3d millennium that most of the towns came into existence they became centers of trade for Egyptian and Babylonian goods. During the 2d millennium, the area known today as Palestine was victimized by invasions by the Hyksos (1720-1710 BCE) and by the Egyptians. Toward the end of this period an African man of GOD and freedom fighter named Moses (Musa) led the Hebrew people out of Egypt, across the Sinai, through the Sea of Reeds a swamp-delta area in the Northern Sinai, incorrectly termed the Red sea and into Palestine. The color of the people during this times was Black. They were in fact African *{Cain H. Felder: Black Presence in the Bible; Jochannan: Black Man of the Nile Excellent sources for Black Presence in the Bible}*

With the destruction of the Northern kingdom of the ancient Hebrews by the Assyrians in 721 BC and the second Jewish commonwealth by Romans in 70 AD.

Judaism would undergo the effects of a culture, a religion and a people in the dynamics of migration. As with all major migrations - especially forced migrations - changes and adaptations were bound to occur. With these migrations, the religion of Judaism was spread west into eastern and western Europe. And with this, Judaism became available to many Europeans. Yeshua {Jesus in Greek translation}, nor Mariam{ Mary}, nor Yuseph{Joseph} ever set foot in Europe, how then could Yeshua be White? It is a sin not to tell the GOD truth!

Adaptations on the part of Hebrew {African} people and adaptations of their great religious beliefs by significant numbers of the people that would cone to embrace it in Europe would cause an alteration of principles by man and strategic maneuvering by Zionist cadre would place many historical distorters in leadership positions that would change the belief of Judaism in the most sinister and sacrilegious way *{Lithanthal: What Price Israel - Brinner: Zionism in the Age of Dictators.}* Judaism was then turn into another belief that is wicked and of the devil; it was no longer Judaism; it was the worship of Lucifer and Zionism unbleached! Like racist capitalism use of slave ships named Jesus - ships that were launched with the blessings of the Pope *{Lerone Bennet; They Came before the Mayflower; John Hope Franklin: Up from Slavery}* - Judaism was used by Zionist as a cover to hide behind and a false justification for naked capitalism, racism and imperialism. The religion would undergo changes for sure! It would find its way to Europe and be susceptible to genuine believers and adherents and also to charlatans, opportunist, sellouts racist, oppressors and worshipers of satan. *{ See: Lithanthal: What Price Israel}*

A significant number of the adherents to Judaism would remained loyal to true tenets of Judaism {remember " originally " an African religion opposed to the subordinating of spirit and substance to law and form. " The Sabbath made for man not man for the Sabbath. **Mark 2:27.** But many more were willing to rebuke the righteous way and were willing to embrace imposters, politicians, ultra-nationalist, racist, zealots, opportunists and political Zionist who succeeded to turn the sacred African religion of Judaism into a pretense and gutter religion of evil. The great prophets of the Old Testament Amos, Jeremiah, Micah, Hosea, and the two Isaiah's were not interested in the restoration of political power. They were concerned with fighting the injustices of their day by appealing to moral values and a GOD of justice and righteousness. They like genuine Jews of today were loyal to **Isaiah 61: 1 - 5**, which in essence says that the Spirit of the Lord has anointed the righteous to do justice and to help the oppressed!

Zionist has used the just religion of Judaism to justify and defend the unjust State of Israel. Alfred M. Lilienthal expressed this point this way:

"So the vast Zionist propaganda machine strives to cement national ties between Israel and all persons of Jewish faith. And sending money to Israel is only a small part of our supposed obligation. The deeper objectives are given by Dr. Margoshes, an executive of the American Section of the Jewish Agency, as being: " – to Zionize world Jewry. . .to establish Zionist

94

hegemony over the developing Jewish communities throughout the world."

The history of the people who through - false propaganda, historical distortions, treachery and lies - are today called Zionist represent a continuous struggle between the truth, and oppressive ideologies that seek to justify an amoral and perverted attempt for world conquest; moreover, by disguising under the cover of Judaism, they give sacrilege to GOD and truth!

The deception was comprehensive!

Thousands of books were published by Zionist that justified, defended and perpetuated the big lie. The Zionist so-called scholars and intelligentsia went on an aggressive campaign to dominate many literary circles, schools and media to continue the big lie.*{Brinner: Zionism in the Age of Dictators}* Even in terms of language the fraud was perpetuated. The Yiddish language, which many people think of as the international language of Judaism, is really the language of Ashkenazi Jews. Sephardic

Jews have their own international language German and Hebrew. **Both the <u>Ashkenazi and Sephardic Jews are those who cannot trace their ancestry back to the area of what is today Palestine</u>**. Most Jews now living in Israel that claim to be Jewish are Ashkenazi and Sephardic Jews. *This is crystal clear proof that these are not the Jews of the time of YESHUA and therefore the state of Israel cannot be the one mentioned in the Bible.*

The legal legacy of imperial powers shows a record of travesty, deceit, and treachery with regards to orchestrated documentation of property, especially the concept of private property and mandated property. The mire concept of private property was unknown to many cultures; this ownership concept is unique to western culture, a curious phenomenon! It was with this imperialist land seizure ploy in mind that the British declared an imperial mandate - by their law - over the land of the Palestinian people with total disrespect for the great indigenous culture of this area; a cultural mix of first African and then the influx, over centuries, of people of western Asia, culminating into what is in modern history a uniquely Palestinian culture right next door to Africa.

The British government decided to endorse the establishment of a "Jewish" home in Palestine, in essence a British fort or outpost in hostile territory that was rich in oil and strategic location. After discussions within the cabinet and consultations with Jewish leaders, the decision was made public in a letter dated November 2, 1977, from Lord Arthur James Balfour to Lord Rothschild- a known devil worshiper. The contents of this letter became known as the Balfour Declaration, which was used as the false legal basis for the establishment of the Settler State of Israel in 1848; an event *of moral travesty that was wholeheartedly endorsed by the U.S. France, Britain, Spain and the major western capitalist powers!* No government that was truly " one nation under GOD would ever do such abominations!

"I KNOW YOUR WORKS, AND TRIBULATION AND POVERTY, BUT YOU ARE RICH AND I KNOW THE BLASPHEMY OF THEM WHICH SAY THEY ARE AND ARE NOT, BUT ARE THE SYNAGOGUE OF SATAN."

3/ Atrocities of the State of Israel

GOD has never blessed an evil empire. The following is a statement made by a Palestinian observer regarding the ruthless and barbaric slaughter that took place during the Gaza horror of 2010. The massacre at Gaza had the full political, financial and military backing of the U. S. government:

"This was nothing more than moral slim and deception camouflaged as liberalism, human rights and justice. You take someone's land, then give it to someone else, and tell the original owners , you are concerned with their civil and religious rights. There is no shame in imperialism only lust, greed and evil intent! The residents of the territory under the British mandate that was named "Palestine" were called "Palestinians. The response of the Palestinian people has been to resist settler colonialism and imperialist a-historical and a-moral laws and mandates. Consequently, from pre Belfour Declaration to the nefarious declaration of the morally filthy

State of Israel, the Palestinian Revolution grew. The following are some significant milestones in that struggle from 1882 to 1948. "

The following are just a small number of the atrocities committed by the State of Israel: barbarism, plunder and murder sanctioned by the evil U.S. government:

1882-1903

First wave of 25,000 Zionist immigrants enters Palestine, coming mainly from eastern Europe. Before this time there is no significant number of European Jews in the area. All that were in this first wave ancestry could be traced to eastern Russia, "the Pale Settlement", Germany and Poland. **Non had an ancestry in the area of what today is rightly called Palestine!**

1920April

Disturbances in Palestine; 5 Jews killed, 200 wounded. British appoint Palestine Commission of Inquiry. Commission report attributes troubles to none fulfillment of promises of Arab independence and fear of political and economic consequences of Zionism. Based on the Skyes Picot Agreement of 1916, the forked tong British promise the Palestinians Palestine if they would side with the British against the Ottoman empire which was a competing imperialist power. After WW2, the British stab the Palestinians in the back and supported the Zionist and the establishment of the State of Israel in 1948

1924-1928

Fourth wave of 67,000 Zionist immigrants, over 50% from Poland, increases Jewish population of Palestine to 16% of total. Registered Jewish landownership (1928) totals 4.2% of area of country. Again, just based on demographics and census records, their small number of immigrants from areas in Europe proves the land did not belong to the settlers. Many church leaders, Sunday school teachers, ministers, pastors and Bishops have no knowledge of the real history. And because of their inexcusable ignorance many a sheep has been led astray.

IF YOU SEE A MISTAKE AND KNOW IT A MISTAKE AND DON'T CORRECT THE MISTAKE, YOU HAVE MADE AN EVEN BIGGER MISTAKE!

18 November, 1928

Second British census of Palestine shows population of 1,035,154-<u>73% Muslim Arab, 16.9% Jewish, 8.6% Christian Arab</u>.

8 May

Conference of Palestinian National Committees in Jerusalem calls for no taxation without representation. Great Rebellion begins

1937 - 7 July

<u>Royal (Peel) Commission</u> report recommends partitioning Palestine into Jewish state comprising 33% of country including Haifa, Galilee, and coastal plain north of Isdud; Arab state in rest of country (to become part of Transjordan); and British mandatory enclaves including Jerusalem. **Part of the Palestinian population <u>to be forcibly transferred</u>, if necessary, from Jewish state.** The Peel Commission was a

joke! Don't believe the British imperialist hype! How can you have a commission set up by the ones who took your land, to decide on the fair distribution of your land to your enemies. How can you be fair if you forcibly remove the original people that were there. ***The U.S. government did the same thing to the indigenous of the western hemisphere with the slaughter and forced relocation of the red people.*** Both Israel and the U.S. are guilty, for they took the lands, changed the name of the land, robbed the resources, and tried to commit genocide and or slavery of the originals inhabitants. This is the truth and anything else in a dam, devilish lie! ***You got to wonder, how many ministers, bishops, Sunday school teachers, deacons and well intentioned Chrstans - have perpetuated the BIG LIE ?***
23 July

Arab Higher Committee rejects Royal Commission proposal and demands independent unitary Palestine with protection of "legitimate Jewish and other minority rights" and the safeguarding of British interests. Rebellion intensifies. The Arab Higher Committed should have taken the position." to hell with the British

102

interest!

September

Arab National Congress at Bludan, Syria, attended by 450 delegates from Arab countries, rejects partition proposal, demands end to Mandate, a stop to Zionist immigration, and prohibition of transfer of Palestinian lands to Zionist ownership.

1 October

British dissolve Arab Higher Committee and all Palestinian political organizations. Five Palestinian leaders deported.

1938 April-August

IZL/Irgun, a Zionist organization headed by Manacan Began bombings kills 119 Palestinians. Palestinian bombs and mines kill 8 so-called Jews.

1939 - 1946
British official estimates of Palestinians killed or executed by British

military and police during Arab Rebellion is over 2,000 for 1936 and 1938 alone. **Total for all years is estimated at 3,500-4,000. About 500 Jews killed in same period.**

In Summary:

We have tried to show **- with substantial reference sources -** in a very brief way a quick glimpse of the true history of Palestine, its earliest inhabitants, and the course of the passive and evil avaricious forces of acculturation that affected this area. **And particularly we have tried to show how this dialectic was intensified to a disastrous level with the invasion of European imperialism and it's most sinister accomplice Zionism. The true history and the understanding of this reality, gives a clear picture to the basis of the struggle that has been commonly referred to as the struggle of the Middle East - an area I chose to call Western Asia.** Within this reality lies the cause of the persistent wars in this area, and also within this caldron lies the answer and inevitable victory of Palestine, Africa, humanity and good over evil!

There is also overwhelming and crushing evidence to the Zionist's military, political and financial backing of the worst crime against humanity and African people, the Atlantic Slave Trade. According to Dr. Leonard Jeffries, 75% of the financing of the Atlantic Slave Trade was supplied by morally bankrupt Zionism who also funded the Columbus expedition to the West and supported the slaves that Columbus had and would have, which were hundreds. [3]

No "good" minister after learning the truth should ever encourage the celebration of Columbus day! Columbus was a slaver, racist and rapist. *{Ivan Van Sertaman: They Came Before Columbus}* But sadly many a minister are ignorant or frauds on this point! Either consciously or unconsciously many push

---

[3] **Page 79 of Bourne, E. G. (Ed.). (1906).** *The Northman, Columbus and Cabot, 985-1503: The voyages of the Northman, The voyages of Columbus and of John Cabot.* **New York: Charles Scribner's Sons.**
Many people are surprised to learn that Christopher Columbus and his men enslaved native inhabitants of the West Indies, forced them to convert to Christianity, and subdued them with violence in an effort to seek riches; Hanke, p. 148.
see Examining the Reputation of Columbus.
In Pursuit of Profits

this lie, even from the pulpit, but unconscious actions still bring misery, confusion and ignorance to many. And those who perpetuate lies must pay for misleading others! **Finally on this subtopic, consider the words of Susan Abilhawa[4] on the massacre at Gaza entitled:**

Palestinians Will Never Forget!

"How can anyone watching Gaza burn escape the bitter realization that history repeats itself? Many have compared Israel's treatment of Palestinians to Apartheid South Africa. But not in their cruelest hour did the Apartheid regime wreak such wanton murder and destruction. Let us stop mincing words. What is happening to Palestinians now whispers of Warsaw and Lodz.

Schools, universities, mosques, police stations, homes, water treatment plants, factories, and anything that supports civil

---

[4] **Susan Abulhawa is a <u>Palestinian</u>-American writer and political commentator. She is the author of the 2010 international bestselling novel, _Mornings in Jenin_.**

society, including the only mental health clinic in Gaza, have been blown to rubble from planes that rain death from clear skies without any resistance, because Palestinians have no opposing air force. Nor do they have an army or navy. No mechanized armor or heavy weaponry. Thanks to Israel, they haven't even had continuous electricity or fuel for the past two years or food and medicine. Israel's siege and blockade of Gaza has prevented the movement of people and goods in and out of Gaza , including the import of the most basic goods necessary for survival.

Half of Gaza children under 12 have lost their "will to live." Can anyone fathom the kind of oppression that leads small children *en mass* to lose their will to live? Israel, and the United States with its unconditional support, will only succeed in radicalizing a whole new generation of its victims of revving world hatred and resentment against this unholy duo. Palestinians will not forget this, as they have not forgotten the past 60 years. But what will you remember a week or a year or a decade from now, when a Gazan, who stood before the long rows of corpses and vowed vengeance? When one of those few million children without a will to live straps on a belt that rips through your daily routine? Will you remember what we did to them? "

Relation of U.S. and Israel (twin evils)

One may question and/ or wonder why one would connect the atrocities of Israel with the United States. My answer! How can you separate them? Another reason is that both the U.S. and the State of Israel play a vital role in the end times prophecy concerning WW111. Moreover, the power and influence of Zionism and Israel inside the U.S. and within other world capitalist powers and puppet regimes is pervasive, and astounding. Zionism is clearly a major form of imperialism, and has played a role in imperialist powers even before the infamous World Zionist congress meeting in Basil Switzerland in 1897, and it has played a major role ever since.

J.J. Goldberg in his book, **Jewish Power Inside the Jewish Establishment** based on data in the early, 1990's, noted that 45 percent of the fundraising for the Democratic Party and 25 percent of the

108

funding for the Republicans came from Jewish-funded Political Action Committees (PACs). No single other lobby including Big Pharmacy, Big Oil and Agro-business plays such a dominant financial role in party funding. Consider the facts from a research paper by James Petras; "The Power of Israel in the United States." Clarity Press, 2006,

p14

> The basis of the [Jewish] Lobby's PAC power is rooted in the high proportion of Jewish families among the wealthiest families in the United States. According to Forbes, 25 to 30 percent of US multi-millionaires and billionaires are Jewish. If we add the contributions to the Lobby by Jewish-Canadian billionaires with assets worth over 30 percent of the Canadian Stock Market, we can realize the scope and depth of the Lobby's power to dictate Middle East policy to Congress and the Executive.

Who Finances the State of Israel?

The question of who is financing the Israeli state is basic because Israel as we know it today is not a viable state without massive external support. As the July 2004 updated Congressional Research Service Issue Brief for Congress titled **"Israel: U.S. Foreign Assistance"** points out in its opening statement: *"Israel is not economically self-sufficient, and relies on foreign assistance and borrowing to maintain its economy. Despite what might seem an insurmountable obstacle not just to Israel's prosperity, but to its sustainability, the country has nonetheless done rather well. Billions of dollars are raised from a variety of Jewish and non-Jewish institutions to sustain the Israeli war machine; its policy of generous subsidies for Jews enticed to settle in colonies in the Occupied Territories and in Israel-sufficient to place the country as the world's 28th highest in living standards for Israel's Jewish citizens."*

Without external aid Israel's economy would require severe cutbacks in living standards and working conditions, leading to the likely flight of most Israeli professionals, businessmen, and recent overseas immigrants. The Israeli military budget would be reduced and Israel would be obligated to reduce its military interventions in the Arab East and the Occupied Territories. Israel would cease being a renter state living on overseas subsidies and would be obligated to engage in productive activity, a return to farming, manufacture and services minus the exploitation of low paid Asian maids, imported Eastern European farm workers, and Palestinian construction laborers.

In the United States there are essentially four basic sources of financial, ideological and political support for the Israeli renter economy:

1. Wealthy Jewish contributors and powerful disciplined fund-raising organizations.

2. The US government-both Congress and the Presidency.

3. The mass media, particularly the New York Times, Hollywood, and the major television networks.

4. The trade union bosses and the heads of pension funds.

There is substantial overlap in these four institutional configurations. For example, Jewish supporters in the Israeli lobby work closely with Congressional leaders to secure long-term, large-scale U.S. military and economic aid for Israel. Most of the mass media and a few trade unions are influenced by unconditional supporters of the Israeli war machine. Pro-Israel Jews are disproportionately represented in the financial, political, professional, academic, real estate, insurance and mass media sectors of the American economy. While Jews are a minority in each and every one of these categories, their disproportionate power and influence stems from the fact that they function collectively: **they are organized, active, and concentrate on a single issue-US policy in the Middle East, and specifically in securing Washington's massive, unconditional, and continuing military, political and financial support for Israel**. Operating from their strategic positions in the power structure, they are able to influence policy and censor any dissident commentators or views from circulating freely in the communications and political system.

<u>Support for Israel from the U.S. government</u>

The data below, compiled by the CRS [Congressional Research Service] Issue Brief in 2004, provide some notion of the extent of U.S. aid and special features.

* Israel has received more than $90 billion in US aid up to 2003, of which $75 billion has been in grants (i.e. no repayable), and $15 billion in loans.

* Since 1985, the United States has provided $3 billion in grants annually to Israel; yet, in the U.S. schools are out of funds, foreclosures are off the hook, over four million in the U.S. are unemployed and millions of children in America are starving; North Philadelphia is one the highest areas of starvation in the country. U.S. citizens are being kicked off of welfare, and Israel has received more than $90 billion in U.S. aid up to 2003, of which $75 billion has been in grants (i.e. no repayable), and $15 billion in loans. **AND THIS HAS INCREASED EVERY YEAR!**

* In 1990, Israel requested $10 billion in loan guarantees, which would enable

Israel to borrow from U.S. commercial establishments, with their loans guaranteed against default by the US government

The following are more examples of non-compassion of U.S. capitalism and reinforces the idea that one cannot be a good president, minister, Christian or person and support the Government of Israel or morally filthy Zionism! The dollar figures given show the abyss of disregard and the chasm of depravity of the U.S. government and the executive office that would tolerate such immorality:

--The money spent on war each day is enough to enroll an additional 58,000 children in head start each year, or make a year's college affordable for 160,000 low income students through Pell grants.

--13 Million U.S. Children go hungry each day! The Cost of one B-1 bomber $200 million. One in six Americans is fighting hunger. In 2008, 17 million households, 14.6 percent of households (approximately one in seven), were food insecure, the highest number ever recorded in the United States. Four million households became food insecure in 2008, the largest increase ever recorded (p. iii, USDA 2008). (To get population figures from family size figures, multiply family size numbers by 2.58, the average family size.)

--In 2008, 39.8 million people were in poverty, up from 37.3 million in 2007 -- the second consecutive annual increase in the number of people in poverty (Census Bureau 2010).{ Also see: Hunger in America: 2011 United states Hunger and poverty facts.

--US unjust war in Iraq and Afghanistan has cost " currently" $864 billion. The cost of two B-1 Bombers (two hundred million) could end child hunger in the US! The cost of the Iraq and Afghanistan conflicts have grown to a staggering proportion of three trillion dollars, but the dollar support for Israel grows geometrically every year.

Some may be critical of what seems to be departure from a spiritual writing. We had to be extensive to make the point concerning the malicious myth with regards to the State of Israel and its twin partner in evil – U.S. capitalism!

10/ THE FUTURE WOULD SEEM FEARFUL TO MANY {Luke 21:26}

Fear is not only a very old tool of tyrants and oppressive governments, fear is also a spirit; a fallen angel that runs very close with the death angel. Remember, all manifest in the spirit realm before it manifests in the earthly realm. We know that fear is not of GOD; for the word of ELOHIM says "I did not give you a *spirit of fear, but of love power and a sound mind*" {2Tim. 1:17}. Fear, an evil spirit is in our movies, and on TV shows. Color coded terrorist warnings are piped to us by the media, and if you follow Homeland security warnings, hidden Taliban are ridding next door to us and riding with us on the subways! Fear is not only profitable; it is an excellent coercive force, but only for those who lack the courage that comes with the graces of **STRENGTH AND GOOD COURAGE!**

11/ YOUTH WOULD BECOME REBELLIOUS AND EXTREMELY DISRESPECTFULL

Revelations tells us that in the end times the youth will be rebellious, disrespectful, more knowledgeable in many ways but definitely weaker. The youth of today have a lot more to contend with than when I was between the ages of 12 and 25. The drugs, the family abandonment, the rape, sodomy , pedophiles and abuse of youth that occurs in the family, in school, and in the church; the movie and record industry which is primarily concerned with profit using fear and control to the cause of promoting sex, violence and loyalty to the state. Indeed, the youth of today have much to contend with, and **its' real name is death, devil and hell!**

> *"For men shall be lovers of their own selves, covetous, boasters, proud, blasphemers, disobedient to parents, unthankful, unholy*

> *2 Timothy 3:2*

12/ MEN WOULD MOCK THE WARNING SIGNS OF THE END DAYS

In many ways, many will say, "for since the fathers fell asleep, all things continue as they were from the beginning of the creation." **2 Peter 3:4**

The Bible says **they love lust** Too many fail to understand that the LORD GOD OF HOST is not a man that HE would lie! The FATHER is not asleep as many foolishly suppose. *GOD is awake and very much alive in the current cataclysmic realities*. To those who are blind , death, and dumb, it may appear that all is well and GOD is detached from the world. Many are

118

blind spiritually and in terms of their political consciousness and; consequently, have no idea of the freight train bearing down on them! The reason GOD may seem to be silent, is because GOD is patiently ***waiting, not willing*** that any perish, but that all come to repentance.

"knowing this first, that there shall come in the last days scoffers, walking in their own lust, and saying where the promise of HIS coming is."
{2 Peter 3:3}

13/ U.S. IMPERIALISM AND THE G-8:

ARE HARBINGERS OF THE
anti-christ and ARMAGEDDON

Many of the prophecies of the Seven Thunders { reference in Revelations } are being fulfilled and will continue to increase in strength and frequency **THE WORLD AIN'T SEEN NOTHING YET !**

Satanically Empowered Control

119

Lucifer cannot bless, but the devil can give power and what may be incorrectly perceived as a gift[5]

Lucifer has been described as the bright star that fell from heaven like broken lighting! A once bright morning star that, due to taking itself too seriously, was cast out of heaven and shattered into a broken fragment that fell to earth and will eventually be cast into the bottomless pit of hell! Many worshippers of satan, " Illuminati, high degree masons, and other wicked people " that bow to the much lesser light, refer to satan as the light and to themselves as being illuminated by satan; in fact the word illuminati is derived from the word Lucifer. The fall of Lucifer has a relationship to the creation of man. After the fall and the expulsion of Lucifer and a third of the angels, ELOHIM creates another being - a little less than an angel - and gives

- [5] **Robert Anton Wilson, called Cosmic Trigger: Final Secret of the Illuminati.- JR - Proofs of a Conspiracy Against all the Religions and Governments of Europe, by John Robison, 1798**
- **To Eliminate The Opiate, by Rabbi Marvin S. Antelman, 1974**

120

this being dominion over the place that Lucifer and a third of the angels fell to. *It is not hard to understand why the devil and demons {fallen angels} hate us, especially we who walk in the spirit of YAH.* Consequently, the aim of satan and his notorious prosody is to defy ELOHIM and destroy the ELOHIM spirit in us, **but only if we allow it**. This strategy of satan has manifested in the *satan inspired political entities of mankind {GOVERNMENTS AND ECONOMIC SYSTEMS}*[6]

---

[6] **Satan, Prince of This World By William Guy Carr; SECRET SOCIETIES AND SUBVERSIVE MOVEMENTS,** Nesta Webster **published a book named Secret Societies and Subversive Movements**

Today, Weishaupt's revised and modernized version of the Luciferian conspiracy is being furthered by the intellectuals who comprise the controlling influence in the Bilderberger Group, the World Federalist Movement, and the Council of Foreign Relations located in the Henry Pratt Bldg., NY. These pressure groups force remaining national governments, and their representatives in the United Nations Organization, to further the idea of "A ONE WORLD GOVERNMENT," the powers of which the Luciferians, not the Communists, nor the Political Zionists, intend to usurp. ever since the fall of humans which refers to the story of Cain and Able. Ever since the fall of satan and the sins of humans, Lucifer has sought to control by way of those in positions of power over others and especially those who rule governments and have great influence over thousands and millions. This fact operated in the evil kingdoms of Moab, Philistine, Edom, Babylon,

These evil earthly powers that will usher in the period of the anti-christ are already in formation; the evil beasts of Armageddon are already formed even if in their infancy. **The current G-8 nations led by the U.S. along with the State of Israel are already following the dictates of the dragon!** Mighty world organizations are in a comprehensive strategy that essentially is not of GOD!

An understanding of the history of the illuminati gives strong confirmation of this. *{such an explanation is not practical to do in this writing, but for a very brief explanation of the history of the illuminati see {Satan, Prince of This World; by William Guy Carr; SECRET SOCIETIES AND SUBVERSIVE MOVEMENTS}*

Such a statement as: "Mighty world organizations are in a comprehensive strategy that essentially is not of GOD!", would appear ludicrous to one that is not conscious, for few know the origin and

---

and Rome and the current evil end times powers and political economies
of today!

scope of powerful world influencing organizations such as Freemasonry, the Vatican, the Masons, Illuminati, the Eurozone powers, the UN, World Health Organization, International Monetary Fund, the World Bank, NATO, the Trilateral Commission, the Federal Reserve System of the U.S. The Israeli Mossad, CIA and the U.S. Foreign Relations Commission.

The people perish for lack of knowledge!

The dragon, which is the devil, gives many world governmental system their power, and great but horrendous authority {Revelation 13:2}. Millions upon millions will experience the oppression of such governments and economic structure because these governments and economic structures are satanically inspired. Daniel {7:23} tells of a world governmental system ruled by the Antichrist:

"The fourth beast shall be the fourth kingdom upon earth, which shall be diverse from all kingdoms, and shall devour the

whole earth, and shall tread it down, and break it in pieces."

The UN, NATO, the World Bank, the World Trade Organization, the World Health Organization, the Illuminati, etc. - all of these powerful world institutions - are exactly what **Revelation 13:2** say they are. They are all components of the developing one-world government - the world government prophesied for the end time over 2,000 years ago!

The New World Order: Prelude to the anti-christ

The prophesied one-world government is being formed on earth at this very time. One only has to look at the formation and actions of the World Bank, The World Health Organization, the UN, NATO, the EU, the Trilateral Commission, the U.S. Foreign Relations Commission, the Illuminati, The U.S. Homeland Security, the Israeli Mossed, world operating organizations and the hegemonic and domineering control and influence of the U.S. within the G-8 capitalist countries and it is clear to see the new World Order has been in effect for some time, <u>and now, it is the priority agenda of the major imperialist entities in the world today</u>. All of this is just a prelude to a major Revelation prediction of a one world government. The Bible prophesies that the anti-christ will ultimately reign over this world government for three-and-one-half years just prior to the second coming of YESHUA in which YESHUA will establish HIS own world government. When? *Soon and very soon!*

The New World Order Prophecy- the role of the Illuminati

The concept of a new World order is not a new idea; it has been around for over three hundred years. Many say that the Illuminati are generational Satanic bloodlines which have gained the most power. A generational Satanist described the Illuminati as "Satan's elite." If the spoken subject of the most powerful secret society were in 1200, the reference might have been to the Knights Templar. The Roman Catholic Church officially endorsed the Knights Templar around 1129; the Order became a favored "society" throughout SO-

CALLED Christendom and grew rapidly in membership and power. The modern day term "illuminati" predominates all secret societies and is a name that adverts to multiple groups within our current era – **ALTHOUH THERE IS A CONTROLING SECTOR.**

Though there is much myth and phony conspiracy concerning the Illuminati, there is a great deal of verifiable proof that it does exist. The Illuminati was founded by Adam Weishaupt who was born on February 6, 1748 in Ingolstadt in the Electorate of Bavaria. Adam's godfather, Johann Adam Freiherr von Ickstatt influenced the young Weishaupt with his so-called rationalism. Weishaupt began his formal education at age seven at a Jesuit school and became the first lay professor of canon law at the University of Ingolstadt. The Jesuit order has a long history of Satan worship and abomination. The Jesuit order was of the main - military wings and secret demonic orders within the Catholic Church, the church that prospered, pleasured, gained power from slavery and fierce oppression of the European poor and "blessed" the death ships of the nefarious Atlantic Slave Trade! *AINT THEY GOT*

NO SHAME[7]

The ruling elites of the early founding fathers - settler colonialist of America were either part of the Illuminati or Freemasons both of whom had the same agenda to enslave and dominate the "new world and to build a New World Order a prelude to the coming forth of the anti-christ! The Occult symbolism of Freemasonry effectively perpetuated the mystery about the Order among outsiders. This amplified the spread of ties to Satanism, alien beings, and the connection to the Power Elite and the secret societies and for this reason the Freemasonry movement of Albert pike was infiltrated very successfully by the Illuminati. The power elite of Lucifer have overshadowed different secret societies in the past! The power elite of Lucifer that controls and directs governments, the world banking system and much of the world's wealth, uses different originations and secret societies to dominate humanity. The correlation with Bible Revelation regarding

[7] **Satan, Prince of This World, By William Guy Carr; See also, SECRET SOCIETIES AND SUBVERSIVE MOVEMENTS, by** Nesta Webster

the characteristics of the anti-christ, the evil
dragon and the actions and projections of the
current G-8 world powers are so amazingly
clear in the current realities of this end time
period that it should shock all into the fear
of the LORD and the truth of EOHIM's
gospel.

Throughout the generations, the power elite of Lucifer have overshadowed different secret societies.

The Illuminati secret society branch
was founded during the year of western
settler colonialism, and consolidated more
with the bourgeois American Revolution.
The power elite of Lucifer that controls and
directs governments, the world banking
system and much of the world's wealth,
use different originations and secret
societies to dominate humanity. Since the
people have an instinctive sense of
righteousness{ the dispensation of grace
},evil must always seek to disguise itself.
*If we saw the devil for what it really is, we
never would sin.!*

The End Time Nations Who they are and their role in the "End times."
A political analysis to help explain a spiritual truth

The Bible prophesizes in many places that, immediately before the kingdom of GOD is established, a world government will rule the earth for a very short period of time. A very detailed description of the last world power that shall reign over the peoples of the earth immediately before the return of **YESHUA** the **CHRIST** is given. The beasts of Daniel's vision, found in **Daniel chapter 7**, bear an uncanny resemblance to nations in our modern world, including the United States- United Snakes! The beasts represent nations that will be in existence on earth when **YESHUA** comes to establish HIS kingdom. If it can be proven that these nations exist right now, if it can be proven that these nations are the major plunderers of the planet, if it can be proven that these powers have in their possession

129

the weapons to annihilate one third of the living population, and if it can be proven that these harbingers of death are the proponents of the mark of the beast and the abomination of GOD, then we can not only show their role in ushering in the period of the anti-christ, more importantly, we can show that the rapture, tribulation and Armageddon are *SOON AND VERY SOON!* Throughout this writing these prophetic axioms have been shown over and over to be true.

Know that we live in the era of the promised second coming and that:

❖ The Coming Financial Collapse in the U.S. and the G-8 powers will happen!

❖ The financial collapse and period of instability and anarchy in countries around the world and in the U.S. will be devastating and create a demand for governmental intervention at the cost of earthly and spiritual liberties!

❖ The Rapture and period of
tribulation will occur very
spoon!
❖ The second coming of
**YESHUA AND THE
FINAL JUDGEMENT
SHALL HAPPEN!**

*"For the day of the LORD is near
upon the heathen: as thou hast done,
it shall be done unto thee."*
Obadiah 1: 15

Modern capitalism has grown out of a
horrid history and legacy of cultural
disrespect, greed, racism, oppression,
exploitation, conquest, invasion and a
barbarism unmatched in the sordid history of
tyranny and anti-people State sponsor terror.
While modern capitalism has accelerated
technology to amazing heights, it has
corrupted itself and morally degraded itself
to the slime of the most depraved toxic
swamp. America is the most technologically
advance society in the world today and at
the same time the most politically backward
society in the world today. The evil,
insanity and dichotomy of capitalism clearly
is in the fact that it feeds on itself and will

131

SOON AND VERY SOON

sell to itself the noose that will be used to hang itself. Historically oppressive empires try to give the impression that they are invulnerable and that their power is uncontestable. Yet, history shows clearly that empires come and go, rise and fall and are eventually brought down by their own evil endeavors, along with the triumphant struggles of those whom they have oppressed. Dr. Martin L. King would never tire of saying, **"The moral arm of the universe is long but it bends towards justice."** History also shows that when oppressive empires fall, they disintegrate astonishingly quick! The American capitalist empire will be no exception to this historical maxim. Not even technologically advanced and "sophisticate" America will be able to stop ELOHIM's condemnation nor avoid its' destiny with history.

The current international financial and political situation of world capitalism is characterized by a large quantity of: destabilization, political-economic uncertainty, military expansion and at the same time military defeat and setbacks, a rising world condemnation and isolation, a growing anti-war movement and anti-oligarchy movement within America and around the world, a decomposition of the " anti-terror coalition organized by America, ground swelling distrust of the American ruling class, a distrust and disrespect for elected officials, devastating setbacks in Afghanistan and Iraq, a razor-sharp growth of mass revolutionary movements in Africa and throughout the Caribbean and Latin America, the growth of an American police state, military attacks on American property and key political figures "inside of America", a critical rising unemployment that is a crisis in the communities of color within America, a deteriorating heath situation among the American citizenry – particularly in the communities of color, intensified racism and racial hatred, the beginnings of a anti-racist, anti-capitalist African and Latino youth movement in the US, American military intervention which attacks popular governments around the world, neo-liberal and neo-fascist policies and an intensification of race-class struggle. Things are not going well for American capitalism, in fact nothing is going right or well for them, and this situation only increases geometrically for the enemy of the peoples of the world. **"CHICKENS WILL**

COME HOME TO "ROOST – *soon and very soon.***"** At the very moment that American capitalism appears to be resilient, at the very moment that the oppressors gives the false impression of permanency and being at their zenith, at the time that international finance capitalism manipulates its media and bourgeois scholars to portray a rose-colored picture of stability and growth, imperialism is entering its decisive period of decline, and empires fall quickly. Let us consider some of the hard, revealing facts of a crisis predicted in the Book of Revelations!

GLOBAL DISORDER

The Humpty Dumpty of the world capitalist system is the United Snakes – with the scorpion of Zionism lurking deceptively within the belly and mind of the beast. The U.S. is the hegemonic power of world imperialism and has the greatest concentration of power, influence and wealth.

Around humpty are little eggs – **secondary imperialist powers** such as

Germany, Japan, Britain, France, Israel, and Holland , and of this menacing assemblage, Germany is destined to take the place of the U.S. There are even smaller menacing eggs – **third rate stooge powers of imperialist**, such as the Scandinavian countries, Belgian, Switzerland, Austria, Italy, Greece, Spain, Portugal, and Canada. There are yet even smaller eggs or **sub-imperialist stooges** such as Mexico, Saudi Arabia, South Africa, Australia, Pakistan, India, Peru, Nigeria, Egypt and a chain of neo-colonial governments and puppet leaders - *a worldwide system!*

Some of these may even dare call themselves socialist, but the spiritual essence and material basis of a thing is critical to understand what it is. It is the position of the masses in relation to power over society that is essential in deterring the degree of socialist development; at the same time genuine socialism must have a clear and active involvement in the fight against world imperialism and for the development of the socialist world; it must bend towards justice and righteousness - and in my view - genuine socialism is in accord with GOD's righteousness! As it is emphasized in the

Book of Acts, "From each according to his ability, to each according to their needs!" {Acts 11:29}, *true Christianity is in direct and categorical contradiction to capitalism and in impeccable harmony with socialism.* Christians must necessarily be in conflict, resistance and in revolutionary hostility to capitalism! The statement by Dr. Marin Luther King is a reflection of genuine Christian principles
.

"We cannot lend our support to an evil system. He who passively accepts evil is as much involved in it as he who helps to perpetuate it. He who accepts evil without protesting against it is really cooperating with it. Non-cooperation with evil is as much a moral obligation as is cooperation with good."

Dr. Martin Luther King Jr.

AN OVERVIEW OF U.S. FOREIGN POLICY
THE ATTACK ON PEOPLE'S SOVERIGNITY

> *" And I will punish the world for their evil, and the wicked for their iniquity, and I will cause the arrogance of the proud to cease, and will lay low the haughtiness of the terrible. "*   *{ Isaiah 13:11 }*

> *" And it shall come to pass in that day that the LORD shall punish the host of the high ones that are on high, and the kings of the earth upon the earth."*
> *{ Isaiah 24:21}*

An accurate and objective analysis of U.S. history and its' international relations squarely places the U.S. at the top of evil empires and shows it to be the harbinger of the anti-christ! The record speaks for itself:

The bourgeoisie American revolution, the Spanish American war, the so-called Indian wars against the indigenous of the Western hemisphere – including the genocidal " Long march and trail of tear" in

137

which over 16000 Cherokee experienced a
forced migration to the west to be placed on
reservations with one quarter to half dying
along the way, the invasion of Africa by
way of the Barbary Coast War, the war with
British capitalism - called the War of 1812,
the racist and expansionist Monroe Doctrine,
the Roosevelt Corollary, the racist-fascist
annexation of the Panama Canal, the
expansion of the Rockefeller oil interest
throughout Latin America, World War One
and Two, the Korean War, the Truman
Doctrine, the U.S. marine invasion of
Trinidad, the Bay of Pigs Invasion, the
invasion of Grenada, the Viet Nam War, the
wars with Iraq and Afghanistan, the proxy
wars and U.S. supplied and financed armies
in Africa and Latin America, the numerous
CIA sponsored assassinations, the overthrow
of Allende in Chili, the overthrown of
Nkrumah in Ghana, the overthrow and
assassination of Patrice Lumumba in the
Congo, the thirty five U.S. backed
successful assassinations that led to a regime
changes - not counting the assassinations
that did not lead to a regime change, the 737
U.S. military bases around the world that aid
the U.S. in the control of humanity's
economic, social and political activities

under the helm of U.S. corporate and military power, and the continued policy of imperialist expansion and war that is endorsed by presidential administration and the hidden hands that controls it. *All of this, and I am sure more that we may never know, give repugnant testimony to the foreign policy record of the United Snakes!* "

---

[8] The Vietnam War began in 1955 and ended in 1975 when North Vietnamese forces captured Saigon. During this period the war escalated from an insurgency in South Vietnam sponsored by the North Vietnamese government to direct military intervention in the south by North Vietnam, as well as the active participation of military forces of the United States and other countries. The war also spilled over into the neighboring countries of Cambodia and Laos. An exhaustive reckoning of the total casualties must include statistical information available for each theater of the war. The casualty figures below focus on Vietnam and exclude those in Cambodia and Laos. The Republic of Vietnam (commonly called South Vietnam) was where most of the fighting took place, and it accordingly suffered most from the war. (See: Vietnam War casualties, from Wikipedia, the free encyclopedia

" Fret not thyself of evil doers, neither thou be envious against the workers of Iniquity. For they shall soon be cut down like the grass and wither away." Psalms 37:1-2

World War 111 and Armageddon
<u>OVER 2 BILLION WILL DIE!</u>

World War III is coming. Most of us were not even here on earth when World War II happened. It was a horrific war. Fifty two million died. In World War I, 8 million died. With the Viet Nam war- over 2millon died.[8] The death toll at the end of 2011 from the wars in Iraq and Afghanistan were well over a million. Millions have perished from wars of aggression and plunder. But in this coming war, World War III, according to an ominous Biblical prophecy, over 2 billion will die. That is forty times the number killed in World War II - **one-third of mankind!** One out of three will die on this planet in this coming holocaust. And when does this happen - *soon and very soon* **- 100% Certainty!** This single cataclysmic event could propel the peoples of the world into the arms of the anti-christ and its one world government.

World War III will bring destruction beyond belief to the human race. In this war of all wars, entire nations will cease to exist including the U.S.! According to Revelation { 9:14 }, the war will originate from the area of the Euphrates River which flows through the Middle East - the region of Iraq, Afghanistan and Iran. With the current tensions in that area{ Russia and the U.S. at present are at a high alert face off with nuclear armed naval forces daringly staring at each other with dueling eyes. And the state of Israel is already making plans to attack installations in Iran, an act that will surely bring in the Super powers to a war in that region. Great Britain, France, the United States, Israel and Germany have pressured Iran, without success, to conform to the will of the United Nations and the international community. In 2011, the president of the U.S. Barrack Obama called Iran an "existential threat to Israel" and says he understands why Israel feels it may need to launch unilateral air strikes to take out the Islamic nation's developing nuclear program. *- soon and very soon!*

DEMISE OF U.S. and RISE OF BEASTS
of REVELATION
The One World government and Un-Holy Roman Empire of the End Times

One of the earliest empires mentioned in the Bible was the kingdom of Egypt. In many ways it was similar to the current United Sates government. Ancient Egypt in **its' days of imperial greatnes**s was vast. The despotic rule of the pharaoh's was broad and awesome in power and influence and many thought that it would be around forever. Its' technological competence was formidable and uncontested, and its military was intimidating with an arsenal of devastating armaments - sound familiar? Its' soldiers were feared and unmatched - that is until the Egyptians did battle with the great *I AM*.

Egypt was not always a despotic empire[9] There was a time when Ancient Kemet was the center of intellect and science, in fact a technological wonder.

---

[9] **Dhiop, Ancient African Civilizations; Jochannan, Black Man of the Nile; Johnathan Jackson, Introduction to African Civilization.**

142

Though hidden for centuries to the modern world as a result of racist interest and Western Asian and European imperial greed and conquest, Kemet(the actual name of Egypt) was the progenitors of mathematics, chemistry, astronomy, open heart sugary, aerodynamics , physics and biology.[10] Inside the grand pyramids of Luxor were found the origins of flying machines and the birth of psychology, theology, philosophy and even monotheism, the belief in one supreme GOD. It was from the ***Book of the Coming Forth by Day***- inappropriately called , The Egyptian Book of the Dead, that we find the written origins of Judaism and Christianity.[11] All this was part of the African Personality that was Ancient Kemet - later called Egypt. ***This legacy of greatness - a shining spiritual testament , fell to earth, like broken lighting***. A major reason for the Kemet fall from grace was the belief by many a ruling powers that they were gods. Thy cut he deal with Lucifer. It was their **arrogance and self-righteousness and capitulation to evil** { a government, and

---

[10] **(Chancellor Williams, Destruction of Black Civilization; W.E.B. Du Bois, The World and Africa.)**
[11] **Jochannan, Africa the Origin of Major Western Religions.**

economic power and society captured at satan's will } that caused Ancient Egypt's decline and destruction. The pride and arrogance that was characteristic of Egypt can be seen in many of today's governments. **Like the super powers of today, ancient Egypt became too powerful for its own good**. There came a time when too many, in too powerful positions, thought themselves higher than the Omnipotent GOD! Thinking themselves wise, they became fools. Too many took themselves too seriously and sought to know not just good but also evil! *And what does it profit a government, a political-economy, a nation, if it gains silver and gold, in fact the whole world and ends up losing its soul!*

The ancient empire of Rome is also a warning of the wages of vanity and State supported tyranny and capitulation to Baal *{an ancient demon of the Old Testament that seduced governments with promise of power and even the bequeath of great spiritual and material prowess to kingdoms that willingly gave up their souls for power, treasures, ungodly gain evil, lust and greed!}* A candid research into the history of the illuminati and Freemasonry reveals that the leadership of both organizations made this same evil agreement with Lucifer!

In our current end time world of 2015 "and current history", the forces of globalization, neo-liberalism and efforts to build a New World Order and One World Government are building a formidable force of evil that surpasses anything done by all the past evil empires combined, a force that - according to Revelation - will usher in the great harlot of Bible prophecy and the anti-christ. The U.S. government and economy will play a major part in this cauldron of abomination and perdition.

As we have shown earlier, the U.S. is currently the leader of world imperialism. The U.S. - for a little while longer - is the international shot caller with regards to world influencing organizations such as; the World Bank, The IMF, the UN, NATO, SETO, the World Health Organization.[12] *The U.S. has the largest stock pile of nuclear and biological weapons. If the concern for the U .S. was weapons of mass destruction, then the forces of Desert Storm*

---

[12] **Dr. Kwame Nkrumah: The Handbook of Revolutionary Warfare .**

should have been targeted towards the U.S. nuclear and biological stock piles. The U.S. - and its major spokesperson, the president - follow the orders of the ruling class and Zionism and are the current great world deceivers.[13] Not only is the U.S. government, Armed Forces and ruling class a deceiver along with being one of the beast mentioned in Revelations; also the U.S. has been, and currently is, the current leader in the harbinger of the anti-christ, but that position of disgraceful and diabolical preeminence is about to be rescinded by an even greater and far more hideous and dreadful world governmental power. The Mystery Babylon the scarlet beast full of names of blasphemy- seven heads & ten horns is alive and will take the world stage, ***SOON AND VERY SOON!.***

Satan has always operated through the material things of the earth in order to tempt and capture humans - the seed of Adam - at his evil, discretion and hateful will. The Apple story of Eve in the garden of Eden is

---

[13] **Gideon Odinga Mukhtar; Obama Drama A Strategy of Neo-Liberal Deception ; also Felix Green: The Enemy: What Every American Should Know About American Capitalism ;G.William Domhoff, Who Rules America**

merely symbolism for material and earthly lust, which is far more than a sexual sin. The fallen angel of perdition, the great dragon as it is termed in Revelation, has consistently sought to extend its' will in the earthly realm by way of governmental power and the political-economy associated with it. Along with this strategy, Lucifer our enemy, has always seduced mankind with lust and pride. As we get a proper understanding of how even, YESHUA was tempted in the wilderness, during the forty days in the desert experience, we learn that satan, our adversary, will promise all the kingdoms of the world and the adversary does have the power to give its' illusive gifts also; very powerful gifts *- to destroy whomever and whatever it may -* but the essential word here is the word, " may.", for it implies actions that can only be derived from " permission." A proper understanding of this speaks volumes! It speaks to the POWER OF THE KINGDOM. But remember, when and if we, as individuals, or we as organizations, governments, armies or even as the forces that are rapidly building the end time One World Government - satan can only capture at his will, which really means *we humans give in* *to that will by our choice.* And this ability of choice discretion - as was explained in the very beginning of the book - was allowed by GOD for a reason!

" Thine own wickedness shall correct the, and thy backsliding shall reprove thee: know therefore and see that it is an evil thing and bitter, that thou has forsaken the LORD thy GOD and that my fear is not in thee, saith the   LORD GOD of HOST. "

Jeremiah. 2:19

Chapter 4

The Mark of the Beast
The One World Government and the One World Church: Already in Existence in Its' Infancy

It is truly amazing and definitely divinely inspiring how the Bible, a book written so long ago, can be so accurate with regards to current world events. The **Book of Daniel, Chapter Seven** is one such

example. In it, we find very detail
descriptions of four evil political/economic
imperial kingdoms or so-called world
powers of the past and a mind-blowing
description of a rising current evil
political/economic imperial power. The four
kingdoms of the past are: the Babylonian
empire under Nebuchadnezzar, which ruled
until 539 B.C., the Medo-Persian empire
(current day Iraq and Iran) reined from 539
B.C. to 197 B.C., the Macedonian empire
under Alexander the so-called great, it lasted
from 331 B.C. to 197 B.C. and the Roman
empire. The Roman Empire ruled from 197
B.C. until approximately 300 A.D.*, but the
evil and demonic force that guided and
inspired it still exists, and surprisingly, the
devil still gives guidance to
political/economic forces that are still in
that area of the world - Europe.* After the
end of the Roman Empire, another empire
was born called the Holy Roman Empire.
The Holy Roman Empire was officially born
in 800 A.D. when Pope Leo III placed the
crown on the head of Charlemagne and
crowned him emperor of the Holy Roman
Empire.

According to Revelation prophecy, an attempt will be made to reform the evil and cruelty of the old Roman Empire into a new and modem form of government and economy. And as we will show, this new form exists in the building of the European Union and the collaborating efforts of the U.S., the State of Germany and the State of the Vatican. A careful study of the Book of Daniel by the "politically/ spiritually conscious" and astute mind indicates that there will be a future revival of this new and modem form of government and economy in the area of Europe. **This revived Roman Empire is portrayed in the book of Daniel**.

Many, even in the church, have said this would never happen; that it is impossible for Europe to ever unite. But an astute look at the current realities shows different. Such false beliefs of many in the church and in the world in general regarding the U.S., the State of Israel and the rise of Germany and the Un-holy Roman empire the Vatican, only serve to allow evil and political/economic oppression to go unchecked. *Remember it was the unconsciousness, naivety and apathy of*

150

***many in the world that was a factor in the
rise of the insidious and barbaric capitalist
State of Nazi Germany.*** Those who are
naive to the nature of capitalism consider
Nazi Germany to be not capitalist but fascist
without realizing that **fascism is nothing
more than capitalism in a crisis** and as a
result, the ruling class uses the governmental
apparatus to maintain control and order and
consequently the State takes on a totalitarian
rigidity of a Police State. The current crisis
of U.S. capitalism will soon cause it to resort
to the same measures. *The groundswell-
rebellious reactions to the draconian
austerity measures implemented by the
European Union in Greece, Spain, Italy, and
Portugal and throughout Europe are just a
screenplay and prelude to the rebellions
that will occur in the U.S in 2015-16.* The
Satan lead rulers of the U.S. are well aware
of this and have prepared for the anticipated
reactions with the Patriot Act and the 2011
passage of the National Defense
Authorization Act. With the decline of the
U.S. political economy and its' hegemony in
the world - **which will become
astonishingly obvious in 2016** - the world
will see the overt rise of the American
Police State and an even more nefarious and

pestilent evil kingdom which has already formed ,a new super state called the European Union. Already it has implemented a common European military and currency.[14]

The number of members that belong to the European Union are now 27 nations and others want to be admitted. Some want to include the North African states and parts of the Western Asia just like the old borders of the Roman Empire. <u>Even though there will be friction and possibly armed conflict to establish itself in Europe, the EU will emerge as a power more formidable than the current U.S.</u> The rise of the one-world government of the anti-Christ is beginning to take its shape as early as now. Its form is hidden in the emerging EU system and the **central controller of the EU system Germany**, along with the un-holy hidden

[14] **THE EUROPEAN RED DRAGON - YouTube: They already have implemented a common European military and currency. They may soon have central government power without sufficient checks and balances to set the stage for the fulfillment of Old Testament and Revelation prophecies.**

hand, the Vatican. The alliance that has emerged between Germany's Chancellor Angela Merkel and the Vatican's point man Mario Draghi who currently presides over the European Central Bank (ECB) is an ominous sign of things to come. The *Economist* even refers to Draghi as Pope Mario.

Draghi's Holy Roman agenda was set *by a group of Vatican elites, operating under the aegis of the Pontifical Council for Justice and Peace*, with release of a memorandum titled: "Towards reforming the international financial and monetary systems in the context of a global public authority." The Pontifical Council for Justice and Peace made a foretelling comment in the statement proposing **"that globalization be regulated by a global public authority.** The ECB may not yet be global, but it does now hold the control of all mechanisms needed to effectively administer the newly developing fiscal union that will prevail in the largest trading bloc on the planet—the European Union!

The president of the ECB, Mario Draghi has consolidated his position as the

second-strongest voice in Europe to that of
Angela Merkel, President of Germany.
Some pundits are even noting that Europe is
no longer dominated by a German and
French partnership. The claim is that any
remaining influence that the French
President once had in the EU leadership had
been quickly seized by Mario Draghi.
Predominant leadership in the EU is no
longer a Merkel-French affair. It is now
dominated politically by Merkel and
monetarily by Draghi, which functionally
transfers into a German Vatican alliance!
Bible prophecy. In fact, considering
Draghi's allegiance to the Vatican, one
could even theorize that the woman of
Revelation 17 is already mounting the beast,
with Draghi now being the singular shot
caller and public voice calling the tune and
applying the arm wrench in the coercive
managing of the European debt crisis.

Rise of the Germany/EU- and the Vatican connection: A Revelation prophecy

One of the major tricks of satan is to
confuse and to conceal. Deception is a

major strategy of Lucifer! The Bible states that Lucifer and demons{fallen angels} **can even take on the appearance of an angel of light**; deception can take on **a " form of godliness."** Many are deceived and confused and many have simply been taught wrong. This ominous and evil strategy, which Lucifer uses, is exemplified even in the interpretation of Bible scripture. Essentially the confusion is in the misinterpretation and misunderstanding of the 12th,17th and 19th chapters of Revelations along with a misinterpretation and misunderstanding of Corinthians 11:2.

  In the 12 and the 17th chapter of Revelation we find mention of a woman. In chapter twelve the woman is described as "clothed in light with the moon under her feet and twelve stars around her head, and in chapter 17 a woman is described as a woman who rides on top of a beast - a great, wealthy **but fallen woman!** The "beast" is a symbol of a kingdom, a political-economic empire. Note in the two pictures above. The picture of the woman surrounded by stars (12 stars) and the picture of the European Union's *flag - no*

accident that it also has twelve stars. {The stars in the EU flag are said to represent all the counties within the European Union. The Vatican claims that the woman in Chapter twelve is Mary- the mother of Jesus. The fact that this woman – thought by the Vatican and many to represent the mother of Yeshua - is portrayed as a European is a reflection of the prevailing ignorance and racism of the Vatican, EU and many more! The **real name of the mother of Yeshua was Mariam and like Yeshua she was an African {See earlier references to The Ancient Hebrews and the Black presence in the Bible}.** All *these false notions are: anti-good spirit, a-historical and wrong to the point of abomination*!

The twelfth and seventeenth chapters of Revelations are two of the most misunderstood chapters in the entire Bible. I was ordained in 2006 and a major focus of the Yeshua Temple of Praise ordination and Bible study focused was on eschatology – the study of end times scripture, prophecies and realities of the end time period. Ever since my pre-ordination Bible study, I have had a robust concern on the topic of eschatology, and still there is much I am struggling to understand. **I thank ELOHIM for the guidance of pastor, Bishop Melvin Brown** for eschatological understanding , particularly as it relates to the twelfth and seventeenth chapters of Revelations. To get a good clarity of these two chapters, Bishop Browns advises that one must have a clear understanding of the following Bible passages:

Fundamental Passages for Understanding

Gen   3.15-Psalms   91:13-1
Corth. 15:25
2Corth 11:2
Romans 16:20 & 13:12-14
Matt 13:43
John 8:12

For clarity, we will offer what we are convinced is the correct interpretation – with Biblical **cross-referenced** proof for each passage and where there is misunderstanding - we will identify the error – and give an accurate interpretation **with Bible scripture proof!** Then, we will return to a clear understanding of the twelfth and seventeenth chapters of Revelations. Even before we deal with what we call "fundamental passages," the first clause in verse one of Revelations Chapter Twelve:

"And there appeared a *great wonder* in heaven"

The two words **great wonder** are quintessential! It means that this is no ordinary reference and that this passage is symbolic and essential in the understanding of Chapter twelve!

Gen 3:15; Psalms 91:13; 1 Corth. 15:25

> *"And I will put enmity between thee and the women, and between thy seed and her seed; and it shall bruise thy head, and thou shall bruise his heal."*
> Gen 3.15

> *"Thou shall tread upon the lion and adder: the young lion and the dragon shalt*

thou   trample   under   feet."
Psalms 91:13

"*For HE must reign, till HE hath put
all enemies under HIS feet.*"

1 Corth. 15:25

This passage {Gen 3.15} has nothing to do with a woman or a woman's seed. Contrary to the interpretation given by the Vatican or the Catholic Church, this passage is not referring to Mariam {the mother of YESHUA}. Many have gotten this false understanding because right before this passage - in verse 13 and 14 - there is mention of ELOHIM's questioning in reference to Eve in regards to her eating the forbidden fruit. One reason there is confusion is because the King James Version has lost much in the translation from the original language Hebrew to Greek. If one read the original Genesis {barasheet- the beginning - in Hebrew}, one would understand that the word Adam in Hebrew *is a plural pronoun for humanity or mankind- the human race. THAT'S RIGHT – ADAM WAS NOT ONE PERSON. In OTHER WORDS* Adam could have been million or billions of people. If *Adam* was not one person, then neither was Eve. Many Christian would find this reality hard to accept because they have been misled for so

160

long. I refer all to the book, "The Pentateuch Haf Torah{*The Pentateuch and Haftorahs: Hebrew Text English Translation and Commentary (English and Hebrew Edition) 2nd edition by J. H. Hertz*}

This is why it is imperative to have some understanding of the original language used by the original writers of the Bible, and the original language was Hebrew and Aromatic. The story of the Garden of Eden and the apple is symbolic and Eve represents the fall of humans to sin.

This has very much to do with the ONE spoken of throughout the volume of the Bible (YESHUA – the WORD and LAMB) of the FATHER, that took on human form{ the WORD became flesh and dwelt amongst us} was crucified, died, was buried and rose with all power in HIS hands!

The woman referred to in chapter twelve is the righteous of GOD, or better the righteous that are saved by GOD and remain faithful to the LORDS will. Consequently, the reference to "enmity between thee and the woman refers to the conflict between the righteous of GOD and Lucifer and those captured or in conscious collusion with Lucifer. It represents the struggle between good and evil. And so, the seed of the women - the faithful of the church - and the seed of the devil must necessarily clash, but good shall win over evil and the church by FAITH, GRACE AND MERCY, will crush evil{ it shall bruise thy head and thou - the devil and demons{fallen angels} - shall bruise her heel! In Psalms 91:13 the crushing of Lucifer {the dragon} and his demons {the young lion and adder} also refer to the defeat of evil. {1 Corth. 15:25} is a compliment proof of the interpretation of the triumph of good over evil.

2Corth 11:2

"For I am jealous over you with godly jealously, for I have espoused you to one husband, that I may present you as a chaste virgin to Christ."

Here the symbolism uses analogies that people can relate to{jealousy and espoused or marriage}. Again the reference to human form cannot be taken literally. This also is reinforcement to the first commandment: *there shall be no other god before me."*

<u>Romans 16:20 & 13:12-14</u>

16:20- *"And the God of peace, shall bruise Satan under your feet shortly"*

This is a reference and confirmation of the correct interpretation *of it shall bruise thy head and you- the devil and demons {fallen angels} shall bruise his heel."* **<u>ELOHIM's word is not contradictory but everlastingly consistent!</u>** If the Bible appears to be contradictory, it is from either a misunderstanding or a false interpretation

13:12-14-*"The night is far spent, the day is at hand: let us therefore cast off the works of darkness, and let us put on the armor of light."*

Here, night and darkness are references to Lucifer and evil and Day and Light are references to GOD - specifically the triune <u>Person of the Holy Trinity</u> - **the WORD (YESHUA, commonly referred to as JESUS).** This same understanding of a " **great wonder** " is also referenced in Genesis 1"1-5.

<u>Matt 13:43</u>

"Then shall the righteous <u>shine forth as the sun</u> in the kingdom of their Father."

This is more Biblical proof that light and the sun are not references to anything natural but to the Divine and Supernatural or beyond natural or material. This point will bring particular clarity and understanding to the reference to the woman analogy in the 12th chapter of the book of Revelation.

<u>John 8:12</u> confirms the above

"Then spake Jesus again unto them saying, I am the light of the world: he that followeth me shall not walk in darkness, but shall have the light of life."

Now, with a proper understanding of the "fundamental passages", it is possible to go into details with respect to the 12th chapter of the book of Revelation.

The woman represents the faithful and righteous church of ELOHIM! The reference to the sun means the church is within and protected by EOHIMs grace, power and mercy. The stars are the angels of the kingdom that guard the church, lest we dash our toe (Psalms 91}. The crushing of the snake laying defeated on the "crescent moon" are references to the triumph of the church over Satan - which is only a deceptive reflection of the true light!

The 12th chapter describes the glorification and persecution *of "a woman clothed with the sun, with the moon under her feet, and on her head a crown of twelve stars."* It is interesting to note the false use by the Vatican and the European Union regarding the symbolism in Chapter Twelve! Here – once again – we see an intentional misinterpretation by the Vatican and its manipulation. On the day of the Vatican's Feast of the Immaculate Conception, the Jesuit son of Rome, Mario Draghi – of the EU, submitted a uniquely conceived *fiscal compact* with the *imperative* that all EU nations sign up to it; a *demand* that was acceded to by all except Britain, which was a knockout blow to the prestige and influence of the British with regards to the EU, Europe and the world! This was just one more significant step toward implementation of an iron-clad *fiscal union,* ultimately to consist of *ten nations* which yield up all sovereign power to one singular overarching authority that your Bible terms "the beast" **Revelation 17:12-13**. Here the Vatican and the European Union unite to deceive. And, part of the deception is to associate themselves with what many consider sacredness, Mary   {correctly Mariam, the mother of Christ}.

     First of all, genuine Christianity does not worship Mariam. *The mother of Christ cannot save anyone and praying to her is not only spiritually futile, it is against the first commandment and therefore an abomination!* This is why the pictures on page 80 are so relevant; **they show the lie and contradiction**. With the proper understanding of the "fundamental Bible passages " indicated earlier, we can detect the deception, and we are not fooled by the Vatican nor the European Union - which according to Revelation - will unite to usher in the anti-christ!

     Chapter Seventeenth of Revelation speaks of the great harlot that rides the beat. Overseeing that beastly power, as its major spiritual influence, is a great church described as a <u>woman riding the beast</u>. There is no dispute with the statement of there being a great church, {large in number and influence} but this church is of Lucifer – **not of ELOHIM.** The two infamous earthly deceivers{The EU and the Vatican} will implement a system - **a One World Government** - which, for a brief moment in time, will literally dictate terms of trade, globally!

The fact that the Pope's man, Mario Draghi, has <u>unrivaled control</u> over Europe's central banking system and the control of the mechanisms that will be used to address Europe's current financial crisis is no accident. The EU Exchange Rate Mechanism and the European Financial Stability Facility is a fait accompli. In an interesting book called **The Rotten Heart of Europe**, *by* Bernard Connolly, it is said that the European Union was only a "cloak for German ambitions**." Germany (*Assyria* in Bible terminology) will be the driving force behind the end-time punishment of America and Britain {Isaiah. 10:5-}** And this force would produce a "king of fierce countenance" **Dan. 8:23**, who would rises to

power "by flatteries" **Dan. 11:21**, and
appear in Germany.

<u>The EURO System: Currency of the anti-christ</u>

With the euro as the center of world
currency, it is apparent that it is emerging as
a leading force in world finance. The Euro
is now the official European currency, and it
will be primarily an electronic currency
where the privilege to buy or sell will be
granted by the State. It is likely that the
Euro will soon replace the U.S. dollar as the
primary world currency as the U.S. goes into
decline. Computer systems have been
developed in Brussels, Germany that have
the capability to manage all the world's
finances and government complexes have
been built in Europe to house a large central
government. The EU is now the largest
economy in the world and the most powerful
political entity on earth.

The euro will have unbelievable
power, and the agenda for its' dominance
has been developed in advance. That global
agenda is constructed around six goals
which is amazingly consistent with what

Revelation speaks of written almost 2000 years ago:

1/The establishment of international economic order (cashless society)
2/The establishment of a one-world government
3/The conquest and subjugation of two super powers (USA and USSR)
4/The ascension of the United States of Europe as the dominant nation in a Confederated one-world government
5/The ushering in of a "supreme" world leader to preside over the new unified One-world government establishment of a one-world religion which will coordinate all the world's religions, cults, faith groups and spiritual beliefs under the guidance of Supreme Pontiff, who will take orders from the dragon which is Lucifer!
6/The New Un-Holy Roman Empire

The ground work for the new Un-Holy Roman Empire is being put in place by the politics of perdition and spiritually fraudulent and reprobated religious figures. *The raptured will not see or experience this abomination, for we will have been taken up in a twinkling of the eye, but this un-holy period, a period when the Holy Spirit will have left the earth also, will be the beginning of the tribulation.* Many will be deceived and run to the sham and fraudulent sting of the beast of perdition thinking themselves wise, billions will be fooled into this enormous " apparent religious awakening." The current naivetés that is characteristic of so many in the world today only gives credence to how much and how many people will be deceived in the near future. Similar to the way a small child is draw to a new video game on Christmas morning, billions will follow the *broad street that leads to hell*. Moreover, this great religious awakening will be the foundation for a universal world church, but this church will be a harlot because it will commit fornication with demonic religions and the kings of the earth who adhere to it. Scripture says that with the help of this "world church" a satanic man will take the remains of the basic structure of the European Union and reform it into the new un-Holy Roman Empire.

This empire will be dominated by 10 nation states which will be divided into ten regional zones and that this power structure will evolve into a world government and it will be initially integrated with the emerging world church that will be head quartered at the Vatican in Rome. A prophetic picture of this merger is given in the book of Revelation in Chapter 17, where the <u>Woman</u> (the harlot world church) rides the <u>Beast</u> (the revived Roman empire). And this will be the mystery Babylon mention as being destroyed in Chapter 18 of Revelations. **The picture above is an EU symbol.** " The stage is currently being set " for this to take place. It is not coming soon it is already here, *and if the stage settings and props are already here then this also means that the rapture will be even sooner*, <u>*in fact it is only a few decades away!!!*</u>

" Therefore deliver their children to the famine and pour out their blood by the force of their sword of their children and be widows, and let their wives be bereaved and let their men be put to death, and let their young men be slain by the sword in battle. "

Jeremiah.18:2 and 23

Chapter 5
The anti-Christ - Armageddon - the
Second Coming

The One World debit card system

The goals of the new world order and the rise of the un-holy Roman empire are coming to fulfillment right before our eyes. We are now in the era of the *"Debit Card System."* This is the final step before the cashless society (the system of the Antichrist).

With this system, a person does not need to bring cash whenever they go shopping. All they have to present is a card with a built in microchip that bears information about **ALL** of the person and **ALL** of their accounts and any info that bears their social security number along with the proliferation of information detected by the numerous Facebook data, cell phone data, e-mail, internet searches, digital TV pictures of you in your home and – only evil big brother knows! This microchip technology is currently in use , as it is built into driver's licenses, access cards, debit cards, and credit cards. This means everything about you can be accessed by the card, and internal microchips(voluntarily or by law implanted }which - as we have shown in the section concerning the signs of the end times - can also modify behavior. **The matrix is real!** This card and/or chip will be scanned by a laser then the amount of our purchase will be deducted from our account. Yes! It sounds so cool, so easy, so convenient, and so modern. Many do not relies with this microchip also there is a GPS system that can track us wherever we are. **Big brother is real, but there won't be any brotherly love!** And it is also the easy way to a life of hell, and then we will die and go to hell.

Here, we give a warning that we know most people will readily ignore: AVOID THE CHIP AS BEST YOU CAN ! AND DON'T GET THE IMPLANT !

Revelation 13:18 Here is wisdom. Let him that hath understanding count the number of the beast: for it is the number of a man; and his number is Six hundred threescore and six. (666)

This system is more evident and widely implemented in richer countries such as Australia which has been on the "debit card system" for more than five years now. Implants are currently being used in Europe, and in the Armed Forces and prisons in the U.S. Also in America a similar system is being introduced in the form of Smart cards and E-cards. **We have previously explained how the chip implant is in president Obama's health care plan and - by law under the Obama care policy - the poor , and those not willing to get their own health insurance will be required to get the implant.**

In January, 1999, the European Union implemented its one currency unit for all the member nations. The Euro will surely become the one world currency by which all other currencies are weighed until they cease to exist. The one world currency is a major requirement for the establishment of a cashless society. Ordinary citizens of the world are so unconscious, so naive and blind *as a bat going to hell*, that they are not aware that the world has already divided into ten magnum regions referred to as kingdoms in Revelations. Regionalization of countries is a step forward to the one-world government. Organizations associated with the New World Order use a " ten kingdom " model in their plan for the coming world government. In the Book of Revelation, the prophet John revealed that the anti-Christ and his ten-nation confederacy will rule the world for seven years during the coming Tribulation Period. Organizations associated with the establishment of a one-world government have already drafted their one-world constitution.

The One World Religion of Perdition is already being formed.
The Rapture must be close!

The formation of the United Religions Initiative 2000, ushered in the One World Religion satanic strategy. It is a reality! In June, 1997, delegates from 100 historic religions and 100 spiritual movements gathered at Stanford University to begin work on the United Religions Charter. Sitting together were Christian ecumenical leaders, Black Muslims, American Jews, Australian aborigines, California pagans ,South African Hindus, Thai Buddhists,

British Baha'is, Catholic priests, Indian Sikhs, and many more religious leaders came together, hundreds of them, many unaware of the deception hidden behind a *semblance of holiness.*

The USA and USSR are yielding their sovereignties to the United Nations due to economic crises in their respective countries. Their governments are coming under the folds of The New World Order.   What awaits now is the establishment, the ushering in of the one "Supreme Leader" to head the one-world government. This is the anti-christ. But according to **2 Thessalonians 2:2-6** , there is still one event that must be fulfilled before the anti-christ is to be revealed, and that is the much awaited "Rapture of the Church." <u>And again we most emphatically say:</u>

If the stage settings and props are already here for the one world religion, the one world currency and the one world government, then this also means that the rapture will be even sooner, in fact it is only a few decades away!!!

Who and WHAT Is The anti-christ

"And now in my vision I saw a beast rising up out of the sea. It had seven heads and ten horns, with ten crowns on its horn. And written on each head were names that blasphemed God."

Revelations 13:1

The beast rising out of the sea *{The sea is symbolic of the mass of people or the people in general.}* refers to the anti-christ which is destined to rise in the last days as the ruler of the One-World Government. This is a person, or group of people, or even - as some Bible scholars believe - a super computer that is controlled by a group of people. Such a computer already exists. According to Bible prophecy, the anti-christ will rule in tyranny and will bring great terror. The anti-christ is destined to be the ruler of the last empire to rule the world which is actually the revived Roman Empire. This empire will control politics, economics, armies and religions of the world. This ruler will be fearless and will not embrace any "genuine" religious conviction; it is of the devil or is the devil. It will demand to be worshipped as God. The real Christians will resist. The anti-christ will persecute and kill many of the genuine Christians. It will force everyone on earth to bear his or its' mark on their forehead or in their hands{ This is the computer chip. } Without this mark, no one will be able to buy nor sell. The revived Roman Empire now exists in our time as the United States of Europe or European Union which consists of the capitalist nations of Europe. *The U.S. government will be the harbinger to the rise of the anti-christ and many in the U.S. will be fooled by a smiling face that will make big promises but will not deliver and such a person already exist!*

Revelation. 18- the Fall of Babylon

Of course, what the devil means for evil, GOD will turn to good and in Chapter 18 to the end of the Bible, Revelation 22, Satan and all those who worshiped and followed it, including those who submitted to the " mark of the beast " get what is coming to them which is defeat, destruction, damnation and eternal hell! **PRAISE BE TO ELOHIM!**

The following is a short synopsis - *in very plain language* - of the Bible from

Chapter 18 to Chapter 22, explaining the fall
of Babylon, Armageddon, the Second
Coming, Judgment and Salvation. Again, I
do not claim to be a Bible scholar, but with
the guidance and the wise counsel of Bishop
Melvin Brown, I know I'm right. Also, it is
in order that I show Biblically, that good
wins out over evil and so this very brief –
and very layperson written account of
Revelations chapters 18 to 22 is needed.
And if it give understanding then, *to
ELOHIM all the glory! HALLELUHA!!!*

Chapter 18 *1-20* *"Babylon the great is
fallen, is fallen and is become the habitat of
devils and there hold of every fowl spirit,
and a cage of every unclean and hateful
bird. "* One of the things that come to my
mind when I read this is New Orleans at
Mart Graie , or Times Square in New York
on New Year's Eve. I heard a joke once,
and I hope you can appreciate the humor. It
says that if GOD did not destroy Times
Square, New York on New Year's Eve -
with all the vice, and demonic carryings on
that takes place there, then GOD owes
Sodom and Gomorra an apology. The
description of Babylon could easily fit the
current domestic situations and foreign

179

policy of U.S. imperialism, along with the G-8 countries, the EU and EURO system, Russia, China, Iran, most definitely the State of Israel and more. Chapter 18 goes further to say that, the world shall receive famine, plagues, and be burned with fire ***Global Warming and Thunder Lighting are just the start.*** It describes the allies of Babylon, *" they shall see her destruction but not come near for fear of the same fate."* Could this be because of nuclear fallout? It says the economic system shall fail. Look at the current crisis of world capitalism today and the inevitable declining economic and political conditions. *Internal turmoil falls on Babylon, the political and economic systems falls and she is hit with nuclear destruction and/ or fire from above, Could this be meteorites or missiles.* ***It also calls on the righteous that have missed the rapture to rejoice in its destruction.*** *Those ministers and unconscious thousands that pledge allegiance to the devil's , red, white and blue flag and all that it " really " represents need to ponder and tarry over Chapter 18 of Revelations. The faithful are encouraged to take an active part in and rejoice in its destruction.* ***Revolution is also an act of praise!***

SOON AND VERY SOON

Chapter 18:21-24 Revelations explains that a righteous angel cast a stone into the sea and Babylon is destroyed. No more true churches left and she reaps what she has sown. *No more churches and prophets are available to help her. A LORD GOD OF HOST tsunami hits Babylon and she is a done deal!.*

Rev. 19- The Multitude in Heaven Praise GOD

And the heavens reverberated in thunderous jubilee and said
" HALLELUHA , SALVATION and glory, and honor and power unto the LORD our GOD, for true and righteous are HIS judgments; for HE hath judged the greet whore, which did corrupt the earth with her fornication, and hath avenged the blood of HIS servants at her hand" { verse 1-2 }

Revelation 19 is one of my favorites in Revelation, it speaks to justice and victory and the complete overthrow of evil; indeed it speaks to the highest aspirations of revolution and spiritual warfare. EL SHADAA, { translated from Hebrew meaning mighty avenger and conquer } Verse 11, " And I saw heaven open, and behold a white horse; and HE that sat upon him was called Faithful and True and in righteousness HE doth judge and make war.

Revelation 19 Verse 13 *"And HE was clothed with vesture dipped in blood: and HIS name is called the WORD OF GOD."* Nineteen describes spiritual revolution. The sons of LIGHT which are of GOD, do spiritual armed struggle with the forces of evil and spiritual wickedness in high places and the sons of LIGHT overwhelms and pulverizes the armies of the devil. And all that worshiped the beast and even those to whom the beast gave great power - those who were deceived by it - were destroyed and hurled into the lake of fire. The rider of victory, the **GREAT   I AM**, with a sword proceeding out of HIS mouth shatters and spiritually incinerates evil.

Rev. 20- The Thousand Years: The great Millennium

Verse 1-3 *" And I saw an angel come down from heaven, having the key to the bottomless pit and a great chain in his hand. And he laid hold of the dragon, that old serpent, which is the Devil, and bound him for a thousand years, and cast him into the bottomless pit "* Verse 4 also says <u>those who were butchered for righteousness, those who did not worship the beast, neither his image, neither had received his mark upon their forehead, or in their hands take part in judging man and fallen angels.</u> It says they judged the unrighteous and reigned with GOD for the thousand years. These are those who really tried to get to glory while they were living on the earth; they tried, when temptation was great ; they kept on praying and having faith when they were at their wits end, they tried when the devil tried its best to get them to lose faith; they stood fast in the liberty which is YESHUA the Christ. **Their good works spoke for them but their faith and grace and mercy saved them.** In other word, they died to the world while the world was trying to get them to live " sinfully large " in it. Although they died to the world, they beard the infirmities of the week while in the world – they were not so holy that they were no earthly good. They did not try to *live large before they died; they tried to die large so that they could live forever - **OH PRAISE GOD!***

They were of the " first resurrection " the resurrection to life over death, life everlasting. They died while they were living; they were - as Romans 8 says - *crucified in Christ and now they are resurrected with Christ, and this made them free from the law of sin and death.*
　　　　Those of the second resurrection are those that " so to speak " partied to death while they were living and when the party was over, satan came and cleaned up their mess and through it in the trash bin of hell. Oh! You don't want to be in that number – *those who will descend to the lower depths of the spiritual holding cell called hell.* But the righteous of the earthly living - despite the afflictions - will reign in the joy of the LORD during the thousand years of the millennium and eventually receive the reward of salvation.

Verse 7-10 Satan is loosed after a thousand years. I use to wonder why would satan be

SOON AND VERY SOON

loosed? If satan is that bad, why not keep that clown locked up? Let me explain it this way. ***Satan cannot capture anyone at his will unless that person willingly place their soul in satan's trap.*** The sinner consciously - by choice - steps into the trap, <u>and satan knows just how to bait our earthly fantasies and desires to make the trap look so appealing and pleasurable.</u> Satan is a master trapper and trickster and deceiver; he is a real dirty pool player. So satan is loosed - **because so many – *by their falling to sin* - are calling for his release.** Looking at it like that makes Revelation 20 real simple and clear! But all demons and those who seek to be with them are judged and cast into the pit at the final judgment.

GOD the father opens the Book of Life and judgment is passed on all those whose name was not in the Book of Life; their names wiped out by their conscious choice to be captured at satan's will. The Book of life speaks to the recording of all our actions. **Nothing escapes the all seeing eye of GOD**. " and they were judged every man according to their works." **Rev. 20:13** You see all that we do and think on earth is recoded. Good or bad, our works goes

185

before us into the Book of Life and remains there until *judgment - nothing escapes, nothing is hid and nothing gets away!* So we must do good works while we can because our works will follow us all the way to glory; they will be waiting for us at judgment! You don't want to have a bad report card at judgment.

"Blessed are them that do HIS commandments, that they may have right to the tree of life, and may enter through the gates into the city."
Rev. 22- Verse 14

Rev. 21- 22 the New Heaven and the New Earth

John says he saw the new heaven and the new city of Jerusalem - the glory, joy and peace of GOD - which could never really be described in words because the glory of GOD is beyond and greater than the wisdom and understanding of men. **Verse 3**, " And I heard a great voice out of heaven saying, Behold, the tabernacle of GOD is with men, and HE will dwell with them, and they shall be HIS people and, GOD

HIMSELF shall be with them, and be their GOD."

" If my people, who are called by my Name,
will humble themselves and pray
and seek my face and turn from their
wicked ways,
then will I hear from heaven and will
forgive their sin
and will heal their land."
2Chronicles 7:14

Why Are People Not More Aware?

Many cannot see the realities and calamities that are all around them; they cannot hear the alarming trumpet; their ears have been deadened by the noise of the world. Many don't see the reality because they have placed too much confidence in the news media that persistently lies and distorts the truth. Many - especially in the U.S. - don't see because they do not read or read the wrong thing; they are politically unconscious and only view the word political in relation to the Democratic or Republican parties which are two factions with the same basic interest and ideology.

Neither have the best interest of the mass of people and in essence both, are a salute to Lucifer {the word illuminati is derived from the word Lucifer.}

Many not aware because they are focused passionately on themselves - a conditioned programmed by: parents that spoiled, schools that encouraged greed and a societal ideology that says the few should live " very good " at the expense and exploitation of the mass. Many are mesmerized by a media driven by profit and avaricious ambition, a tool to control the masses – a tool owned and operating in the interest of the few! "Back in 1983, approximately 50 corporations controlled the vast majority of all news media in the United States. Today, ownership of the news media has been concentrated in the hands of just six incredibly powerful media corporations. In the U.S. , these corporate behemoths control most of what is watched , heard and read every single day. Corporate behemoths own television networks, cable channels, movie studios, newspapers, magazines, publishing houses, music labels and even many of our favorite websites. Sadly, most Americans don't even stop to think about who is feeding them the endless hours of news and entertainment that they constantly ingest. Most Americans don't really seem to care about who owns the media. But they should! The truth is that each of us is deeply influenced by the messages that are constantly being pounded into our heads by the mainstream media. The average American watches <u>153 hours</u> of television a month. In fact, most Americans begin to feel physically uncomfortable if they go too long without watching or listening to something on TV; it's a shame thy don't feel the same way about the Bible. Sadly, most Americans have become absolutely addicted to news and entertainment and the ownership of all that news and entertainment that many crave is being concentrated in fewer and fewer hands each year.

Six corporations collectively control U.S. media today : Time Warner, Walt Disney, Viacom, Rupert Murdoch's News Corp., CBS Corporation and NBC Universal. Together, the "big six" absolutely dominate news and entertainment in the United . When you control what Americans watch, hear and read you gain a

great deal of control over what they think.
They don't call it "programming" for
nothing![15]

Those who would see the truth, those
who would dare to be conscious and
organized are terrorized by a government
that has vowed to protect the ruling class
and submit to the clutches of Lucifer! In
other words, many have decided to choose
the will of the devil instead of the will of
GOD! **And woe to them who do!**

Events of great consequence and
world altering magnitude are unfolding on
the world scene around us. *Occurrences of*
magnitudes never experienced before are
popping off and a sleeping world is so
anesthetized by the razzmatazz of the
current societal nonsense that many have
no clue at all as to the spiritual times we
are in! Like the proverbial frog in the pan
of water that is slowly reaching the boiling
point, millions are just floating by with no

---

[15] Ben H. Bagdikian, The Media Monopoly, Sixth
Edition, (Beacon Press, 2000), Ibid; Who Rules America

inclination of the impending doom! It is said that ignorance is bliss and this may be true in some instances, but when ignorance leads to eminent destruction, it is foolish to " perish for lack of knowledge." In most instances there is no good excuse not to have heard and to adhere to the word of GOD. Many have consciously chosen to ignore GOD. Too many have decided to tell GOD, I hear you but not right now, or I know LORD, but I will obey you tomorrow; not realizing that tomorrow is here and we are on the precarious edge of the end of times! When one steps outside of GOD's grace and its protection, evil is right there waiting. Why run from a strong tower in the midst of an attack! And, the devil is always on the attack seeking whomever it can devour!

Straighten Up Inside Before You Try to Evangelize Outside: Contradictions Within the Ministry and the Church

The Bible says that there is only one church and one body that Jesus calls his people to. **Colossians 3:1** And actually there is only one gospel which is the word of GOD. We of the YESHUA Temple of

Praise, in Philadelphia, Pa. are non-denominational. There are many beliefs and many denominations, but only one church and that is the church of the first born of YESHUA the CHRIST. **Hebrews 1**

   Some might find it quite difficult to discover the true remnant church. There are over 1,000 different churches and organizations in the world. Almost every one of them claims to be GOD's church, but they all have differing beliefs. But GOD wants one gospel and one church. If the church is the one body of CHRIST **- and the true church is -** then, we should be obedient and not strike off and strike out on our own self-righteousness, building churches of our earthly desire and opportunistic cravings! All this leads away from **" the way, the truth and the light",** and consequently, are not of GOD! The end time realities will be such that many will be forced backed and scared back into the true fold; it will either be GOD's way or perish! The devil and the world will not be victorious. GOD's word says that "I will build my church, and the gates of Hell *(antichrist empire, G8 or any other evil)* shall not prevail against it." And for those who stand fast in the liberty of the

SOON AND VERY SOON

true light, the *WORD* says, I will give you
the keys to the kingdom of heaven, and
whatever you bind on earth will be bound in
heaven, and whatever you loose on earth
will be loosed in heaven.
Matt. 16:18–19.

The true church will stand tall and bold in these end times. They will be like JESUS - who was no punk!

And for this spiritually and earthly
courageous act GOD says that HE has
special favor **Joel 2:29** and the gates of Hell
(antichrist empire) shall not prevail against
it; for those who are in in YESHUA the
CHRIST, there will be no condemnation!
Romans 8: 1

This is certainly not to say that the
righteous remnant won't be attacked. The
Bible says that satan will come at the neck
of the true church, even attacking like a
flood but that **THE LORD GOD OF
HOST** will raise up a standard against it ,

and never have the righteous been forsaken! So in these end times not to have courage is not to have faith. *Not to oppose and speak out against injustice is to punk out!* The true church must be strong and of good courage! We must stand fast in our impenetrable liberty and be willing and zealous to stand up as the Hebrews men of valor did and refuse to bow to the nonsense of the current world. We must stand up to the anti-christ empires and those who are captured by its evil will. This is an issue of sanctification and by that a **willingness to separate from the world** - in a sense - while at the same time involving ourselves in the world as Lot involved himself in Sodom and Gomorra. Sanctification does not mean to stay in the house or stay in the confines of a church building, but to get out into the street, the highways and byways and teach, preach, organize and do the good word and the good work! **"HE"** was a people person; YESHUA spent very little time in a building or in the temple. The church must stand up to a world that hates it. The church must stand up to political tyranny and to political oppression, even to the G-8 anti-christ countries and governments. The church should be on the front lines of the just political strugglers in the world and even on the front lines and ramparts of just social revolution! The church must stand tall and let our light shine and our salt flow, that the world may see our light and taste our salt and **TO GOD BE THE GLORY!**

Even in the schooling and training of many younger ministers, evangelists and church officials nowadays there are glaring contradictions. Many have been programmed in school and in the popular culture to be relativists and apologist for an unjust government and economic system! Well, for them, judgment will start at the pulpit and at the alter! Weak liberalism abounds and capitulation to the wrong authorities. Many a minister and pastor are more loyal to the lesser light instead of thee LIGHT. While they seek after the pleasures of Masonic halls *- that in many instances are just the pretense for satan's orgies and secular governments conspiracies*! Many a minister and pastor are too fearful of government - and the loss of secular " faith based " funding - to stand fast in the liberty and courage of GOD's grace. Too many a minister and pastor are too fearful of

195

breaking U.S. law, *but when man's laws goes against GOD's law , then it is righteous and an act of praise to be an outlaw!* But what will they do when the government says all must wear the mark of the beast? What will they do when the government orders the audit of all actions of the church? What will they say when the government outlaws the Bible? What will they do when the government says they must marry gay couples. Will they swing fits like Samson or will they sellout like Judas? Too many so-called church leaders are as lukewarm as the Laodiceans **Rev3:14-22** in our attitude to church responsibility and Bible prophecy. Too many refuse to challenge the unjust laws. Too many do not read the Holy Scriptures with understanding and far too many do not walk in devotion in submission to GOD! Too many are cowards to the current baals of the day. **But they must remember that judgment will begin at the pulpit. And the righteous will be ordered to swing the Josiah ax without pity and without mercy! AND TO GOD BE THE GLORY!**

"And I will punish the world for their evil, and the wicked for their iniquity, and I will cause the arrogance of the proud to cease, and will lay low the haughtiness of the terrible."

Isaiah 13:11

"For the day of the LORD is at hand; it shall come as a destruction of the ALMIGHTY. Therefore shall all hands be faint and every man's heart shall melt: and thy shall be afraid: pangs and sorrows shall take hold of them: they shall be in pangs as a women travaileth: they shall be amazed one at another; their faces shall be as flames."

Isaiah 13:6

Chapter 6

WHAT MUST BE DONE?

Will the real church **Get Up and Stand Up for GOD's righteousness?** Soon and very soon, we will find out who the real church is. The true church of GOD will not be the ones in the designer pastor robes or the churches with the fleet of air conditioned vans or the praise dance group with the superb rhythmic steps and mime theatrics to match. The true church won't be the winner of the " we the best denomination out here award " or the one with the largest " faith based grant from questionable donors and right wing fanatics and government controllers. The Bible says that there is only one real church or body of Christ and that is the Church of the First Born of Jesus Christ. **CFBJC Colossians 3:15**

Some might find it quite difficult to discover the true remnant church. There are over 1,000 different churches and organizations in the world. Almost every one of them claims to be God's church, but they all have differing beliefs. The real church will be identified by the evidence of their walking in the spirit and by the fruits of their labor. **They will be *the Living Epistle of GOD and the earth, and demons shall know them!*** There are three Bible quotes below that point out the power and responsibility of the true church and offer a guiding light to what we of the { **CFBJC** } must be about in these Apocalyptic days.

" I will build MY church, and the gates of Hades (Antichrist empire) shall not prevail against it."

" I will give you the keys of the kingdom of heaven, and whatever you bind on earth will be bound in heaven, and whatever you loose on earth will be loosed in heaven."
Matt. 16:18–19
" Every valley shall be exalted, and every mountain and hill shall be made low: and the crooked places shall be made straight, and the rough places plain and the glory of the LORD shall be reveled and all flesh shall see it together."
Isaiah40:3-5

The True Church Must
Reach out to the lost now

The challenge is for the Church to reach out to the lost now. No government in the world has the complete answer and without GOD nothing can really succeed. **Politicians, scientists and or even military power cannot save us but the gospel of YESHUA Christ can, and GOD in HIS wisdom and righteous can even guide each culture to the most effective political ideology**. The church is commanded to go forth with strength, confidence and good courage. We of the church are confident in GOD's word that, where the spirit of the LORD is there is liberty, and with this liberty comes power to correct injustice, to bring aspects of truth to lies, to right wrongs, to reach high into the heavens and bring low the glory, insight and revelation of ELOHIM, even to defy natural law and governmental laws that are unjust! The LORD is sovereign, consequently, when acting in the will of GOD, we are above earthly and manmade law and if necessary we are to correct and even overturn governments as the early Hebrews did with the corrupt governments of Egypt, Edom, Moab and the Philistines! **Revolution is also an act of praise!** Neither the power nor the wisdom of man will ever be greater than or defeat the power of GOD!

Be Witnesses to the Ends of the Earth

Our role - especially in these end times - is to witness to HIS righteousness and to joyfully manifest the fruits of the spirit " to the ends of the earth." **Acts 1:8 A spiritual witness is not one who stands by and observes. Witnesses are not neutral on lookers or just record keepers and chroniclers of injustice**. A true witness is an active agent for justified change; they are doers of the word and not just speakers of it. Like it is mentioned in the Book of Job, a witness is one who abhors injustice. A witness would speak out and act out against the injustice of the predatory wars of the U.S. in Afghanistan, Iraq and Syria. A true witness and true witnessing pastor and church would pour the congregation in the streets to protest against racial profiling and police brutality; a true witness would oppose same sex marriages and the genuine witness would be opposed to U.S. and all capitalism with the same zealousness that opposes abomination and reattributed sin!

The Importance of Evangelism

Evangelism is the order of the day! The remnant and righteous of GOD must go out into the wilderness and bring the GOOD NEWS! It must be done in Faith, in Word and in deed. We must be the John the Baptist of this age! YESHUA spent very little time inside of the temple. HIS ministry was more of a street and outreach ministry. Most people will not come to church, so the church must come to them. If HE came to us, then we must go to them **- in HIS name!** I learned, as an organizer, when you go to the people, go well informed, welled trained, dedicated and very humble. Your humility must be your strength and your faith and integrity your greatness and motivation! You cannot go to the wilderness with an attitude of " I am holier than thou." Too many have been turn away from GOD by self-righteous evangelism. They have run people away and once they leave, it is an arduous task to get them back. We must act like good ushers and great gate keepers, and we must act LIKE WE KNOW; first impressions are so very important. **Let us not be so holy that we are no more earthly good!** Let our light go forth when we evangelize, and let us decrease so that YESHUA can increase in us.

Guard Against Self-Righteousness

How can you say you love GOD - whom you can't see - if you are hypocritical and hateful to your neighbor - who you see every day? How can you shout out Halleluiah in church and the next day curse out your neighbor or ignore the oppression that exists under systems of oppression and exploitation? Vanity and hypocrisy are not of GOD! Yet, these earthly burdens weigh us down and thereby keep us from rising to the occasions of life that gives us blessed opportunities to be the salt of the earth and the LIGHT of glory to others. We must never be so holy that we are no longer any earthly good. Self-righteousness comes to church every Sunday without fail; it parades down the broad street that leads to hell. It promenades across pulpits and sits high in choirs, and it stands as an abominable sentry at the door of GOD's righteousness, blocking and discouraging those who are seeking the LIGHT. In these end times, the devil will try to use **self-righteousness** against the saints of GOD. The *" I am more holier than thou attitude "* has wrecked devilish havoc in the body of Christ. Let it never be a part of your spiritual personality. *We must decrease if we want to increase in GOD's grace and power. The last shall be first!*

Not Pruning the Bush
Thereby Stunting Its Growth

The word of GOD will convict, and it will cut deep even to the dividing of mind, body and spirit. Necessary surgery can be so painful that anesthesia is required. **Pain is sometimes the best way to bring about pleasure and at times the best way to rectify**. My parents, when they spanked me as a child would sometimes say, " this is going to hurt me more than it will hurt you." Well, at the instance of the beating, I found this very hard to believe; in fact, I use to think, " they got to be enjoying this, for they are doing it with such zealous." Of course, I was confused. There are times when we cannot spare the rod of principled criticism and blistering warning. There are times when we must judge - *just judge righteously and start with ourselves.* A chastisement is not necessarily a curse. Sunday school lessons, prayer meetings, church meetings, sermons and pastoral and church counseling should focus sessions on how to give and take principled constructive criticism. And, a crucial aspect of criticism training and education must **highlight as a matter of principle** that no one is above criticism because no one is perfect, for we all have fallen short of the glory, and we all have room for improvement! There is a dangerous elitism that exist among many Christians, pastors, ministers and church officials. Too many think they're above criticism. The only ones that are above criticism are those who made it to glory!

Be the Living Epistle

In our Bible study at the YESHUA Temple of Praise, Bishop Melvin Brown always encourages us to *Be the Living Epistle!* For many people our " righteous walk " will be the only Bible that many will read or have access to. We must walk the walk that we read and study about.   **James 2:14-22** The minister that " says " what to do, can never be as powerful as the minister that practices what they preach.   And we all are called to minister. We must be willing to be broken bread and poured out wine. We must offer ourselves up as a living sacrifice, holy and acceptable of the spiritual responsibility, for after all this is our job. We have been sent out into the wilderness to save and to serve. And even when the people we serve spit in our face, we must be strong and of good courage and ironed willed enough to wipe it off and continue in service. **This does not mean we are to be a fool**, nor does it mean that we should bless dogs nor cast pearls among swine, for both will trample our good intent and not appreciate our good grace. *Meek don't mean week or to be a fool!*   At times being the Living Epistle, means that we will have to *put out foot up the assets of people - in the name of JESUS*. Just make sure you pray before you act, so that you act in accordance with GOD's will!

Consider the Whole Matter

Just a cursory and a *" politically-conscious "* look and analysis of **current world events and political economic trends** along with a view of **Bible revelation prophecy**, shows a consistency, a harmony and a correlation between the - *"politically-conscious and spiritually conscious."* - This marriage of harmony should give one a disquieting recognition that big world changing events are in motion and moving towards a traumatic and apocalyptic climax! But to see this, one must read far beyond the Bible; one must be conscious of world events and have a correct political understanding of such events. Politically unconscious ministers and Christians make for poor leaders!

Initially, this small book was written in the last month of the year 2012. Since its' initial writing, we has seen ecological devastation - much of it caused by a disrespect and disregard for humans and nature primarily by multinational corporations. Since its' initial writing , the world events – natural and political have been astounding. There have been ravishes of unprecedented famines and predatory wars that have left in its wake murder, mayhem, mutilation and devastation largely as a result of a capitalistic insatiable appetite for power, profit and unholy conquest. The devil has been very busy in these last days. **But these horrors and shocking events are about to be surpassed by events that will dwarf anything that the world has ever witnessed before.** But again, GOD would not have us ignorant, and these events are spoken of in the Biblical books of end time prophecy. And, when we see these Armageddon predictions unfold, know that the rapture and post rapture, tribulation including the rise of the anti-christ, and ultimately, *THE SECOND COMING,* are unfolding and occurring if not currently then undoubtedly - *soon and very soon*!

The crux of this book can be stated in two major themes:

1. to encourage the reading of GOD's word and adherence to GOD' commandments. For if we love HIM, we will struggle to obey. Notwithstanding our earthly weaknesses, GOD knows our hearts and our sincerity or lack of it.   In preaching and ministering, I often tell people that heaven is filled with former big sinners who really made a sincere effort to get there, AND MADE IT!

2. That the rapture is real, it will happen and it will happen soon! No doubt one of the most specific, startling and we hope GOD fearing future statements we will make is that looking at the world and all that is taking place, and considering all that has been said and shown in this book should give ample evidence that **there is a - great possibility - that the rapture will occur within the next ten to thirty years, that would be by or before 2033!** If we are wrong in this, then there is no real damage done, for at least we have made a strong and convincing argument for number 1. But if we are right, then the best we can say is:

"Seek ye the LORD while HE may be found, call ye upon HIM while HE is near: let the wicked forsake his ways, and the unrighteous man his thoughts: and let him return unto the LORD, and HE will have mercy on him; and to our GOD, for HE

will abundantly pardon." **Isaiah 54: 1-7**

"A thousand shall fall at your side, and ten thousand at your right hand; but it shall not come nigh you"

Psalm 91:7

SEE YOU IN THE RAPTURE!

Chapter Seven

A PRAYER FOR SPIRITUAL WARFARE

All mighty GOD, merciful and gracious, long suffering and abundant in goodness and truth, GOD that bestows mercy for billions, LORD that forgives our iniquities, transgressions and our sins; GOD that will in no way and by no means clear the guilty that willfully transgress against thee and come against your elect! In the name of YESHUA and by the sacred blood, we pray that we now find grace in your sight. We claim the covenant given to Abraham, and with earnest expectation we receive the favor that was predestined for the elect, given to us before the foundations of the world. We bless your name FATHER GOD, and we prostrate before you. We totally decrease that you may increase in us to do your will for your glory. Omnipotent GOD and Supreme Potentate, speak through us, glow through us, and organize through us. By your word and grace, use us to work miracles for the FATHER to be glorified, and by the blood of the LAMB and in the name of YESHUA, we ask that you hear and grant this prayer request.

FATHER GOD, build us up spiritually. Guard us against being hypocritical and guard us against hypocrites. In the midst of tribulation, let us know that suffering is redemptive and let it be so GOD. Help us to stand firm in all situations to be an example and rock for others. Use us LORD to be a fountain to give living water to others. GOD of the Seven Stars, Ruler of the seven heavens, King of the universe, the heavens and all worlds, bless us with revelations that we may minister greatly for you Glory LORD. LORD GOD OF HOST, work in us your mighty grace. Give us a mighty spirit of patience. Shape us and use us as your tool and rod. Keep us from temptation. Let your Spirit be in our thoughts, and actions; let your grace be a fortress to prevent evil from entering our thoughts. Cast out all evil before us, around us and block its entrance within us, in the name of YESHUA, we pray!

LORD , In the name of YESHUA, as you have called, anointed and chosen me as

your manifested , I ask for your grace and
power to have authority over all devils and
to cure diseases, to preach the gospel, to heal
the sick, all for your glory LORD. I look to
your love and grace to provide all my needs
and to answer this prayer request. By the
blood let it be. HOLY SPIRIT, by the
power of the FATHER, give me inter-
cessionary favor to pray for others and
through your grace and mercy, to bless
others in the name of YESHUA and by the
blood; I request; I speak it. HOLY SPIRIT,
make me swift to hear, slow to speak, and
slow to wrath. Reveal to me and in me the
engrafted word and help me to be a
consistent doer of the WORD! LORD I ask,
In the name of YESHUA and by the blood,
that you Bless me as you blessed the
disciples, that through your grace miracles
are performed and the sick are healed. Place
your spiritual force in me LORD that I may
have life in your glory and at the end of this
earthly life to have life everlasting. In
periods of tribulation and when my enemies
come against me, HOLY SPIRIT, be my
rock of defense and my rod of victory.
Abide in all I do LORD, my thoughts and
decisions that my joy will be fruitful.
LORD, let your grace be a fountain in me

that provides spiritual nourishment to others and a guide for other to consciousness and salvation. Fill my spirit and my body with your glory that I may connect to the spiritual umbilical cord of the Kingdom and receive nourishment from the throne of your glory, for your glory FATHER GOD. Fill me with the compassion of the lamb of GOD that I always am sensitive to the suffering and needs of others. Teach me, strengthen me and guide me to be a guide to the harvesting of souls. Lead me to bring your glory to all and to be a liberator of my people and to humanity. LORD I ask, In the name of YESHUA and by the power of the supreme spirit of truth, and in YOUR mercy, quicken me to always walk according to the Spirit and never to be vain, arrogant and non-appreciative to others who have helped me. Use me for your glory LORD and I rejoice in the spiritual liberty that you have given me and I will use it for the glory of the FATHER. Let the cloud of your glory descend on all I do and wherever I am, that the FATHER may be glorified. Use me to bring edification to others. Bless me and teach me that I always walk as a child of light and the salt of your glory. Let me receive the fruit of the spirit in all goodness and righteousness. Place your spiritual force in me and all I think, write, organize and do. Anoint me that evil strong holds are broken and allow me your grace, OH! LORD GOD OF HOST, to break evil strongholds, for the glory of the FATHER. Let my strength always be in your Spirit and joy.

HOLY SPIRIT be my guide and pray for me. Bless this earthly house and help me with my earthly limitations and have mercy on me in my earthly weaknesses. Let the light and power of the HOLY SPIRIT glow and grow strong in me. Let the power of the resurrection be in me to reveal the glory of the FATHER to convince all in doubt. Let me never be without your glory that I will always be spiritually productive and faithful in the mission you have given me FATHER GOD. LORD I ask, In the name of YESHUA and by the blood, let me always be salt and light to the least and to those in need a mighty advocate, avenger and organizer for the spiritually bankrupt and the oppressed. Let the light of your glory always shine in and around me and your glory in me be seen of all, that the FATHER may be glorified. Give me the strength and courage to suffer great things for your name sake and for the conversion of a great number, all for your glory FATHER. LORD, I totally decrease that you totally fill me with the power of the kingdom for the glory of you FATHER GOD. Wherever I cast my net, my intentions, my prayers, my efforts and my intercessions for others and for my family and the organizations that I am a part of, for all I think and do, let me be fruitful in abundance and let miracles go forth for the glory of you FATHHER GOD in the name of YESHUA and by the blood, I PRAY!

Great and omnipotent GOD, that is greatly to be praised, let the power of the kingdom flow through me, through YESHUA THE CHRIST our savior, that I stand firm in faith to be always triumphant over the devices of the evil one. Abide in me HOLY SPIRIT that I do good and great in all endeavors that the FATHER may be glorified, that conversions go forth, that the elect of the supreme throne be edified and encouraged and for the building of the church and the perfecting of the saints. Guard me from all condemnation and let me always walk in your glory that sin in my flesh be condemned. Keep me spiritually minded and in your peace YESHUA. Let the spirit of resurrection quicken all I think and do giving me the right of HOLY SPIRIT inheritance. Let your glory be revealed in all I do and manifest all around me for the glory of the FATHER. HOLY SPIRIT SEARCH MY HEART AND MAKE INTERCESSIONS FOR ME AND ALL I DO AND LET YOUR IMAGE ALWAYS BE IN ME AND SHOW IN ALL I DO. LET IT BE IN MY WAKEING HOURS, IN MY DEREAMS AND IN MY SPIRITUAL TRAVELS. LORD I ask, in the name of YESHUA by the blood and HOLY SPIRIT grace me to cleanse myself from all impurities and to teach and help others to do the same. Help me to learn good things from others. Guide and instruct me to deceive none, corrupt none, and to defraud none. Grace me to be a great in speech, thought, preaching, ministry, writing, organizing, for your glory LORD. Bless me to be exceedingly joyful in all tribulations knowing that you FATHER GOD are my rock, buckler and salvation a very present refuge and help, because you love me so LORD! Let me bring comfort to those who are spiritually, mentally and physically depressed and courage to those who fear, liberty to those who are oppressed, knowledge to those who are ignorant, hope to those who are hopeless, a friend to those who are in need of compassion and a mighty minister to all for the glory of the HOLY TRINITY, **in the name of YESHUA , by the blood, in the name of the Holy breath of the GOD, by the promises of ABA FATHER , FOR THE GLORY OF ELOHIM , I pray and look forward with earnest expectation and by your power , I speak this pray to reality - It is so, turda rabbi and AMEN! AMEN! And AMEN!**

SEVEN STEPS TO GOD's FAVOR

**Complements Of
YESHUA Temple of Praise: Bible Study Class
Bishop Melvin Brown
YESHUA Temple of Praise. Philadelphia, Pa.**
yeshuwatempleofpraise@yahoo.com

1/GODLY INFLUENCE (Gen.39; 2-3) – (James: 1-2)

Brings forth the drive to "do"! GOD will confirm and provide a way out of tribulation!

2/BUSNESS FIDELITY- UNMERITED FAVOR (Gen. 39:5- 6

GOD'S grace is sufficient

3/RESISTENCE OF TEMPTATION (Gen.39:7-20)

GOD will provide a way out and escape from temptation!

4/DIVINE FAVOR (Gen:3921-23)

We will be poured out a blessing we will not have room to receive; it will overflow on others!

5/PROVIDENTIAL CIRCUMSTANCE (Gen:39,40,and 41)

By way of who you are and your gifts, GOD will perform a good work in you.

"For it is GOD which worketh in you to will and to do of His good pleasure" (Philippians 2:13).

6/HONORING GOD (Gen.41:16)
To GOD be the glory

7/DIVINE REVELATION (Gen. 41:25-36)
Supernatural communication from God to man
****

END TIME GLOSSARY

It is my prayer that this book reaches an audience that is either ignorant of the Bible or have given very little attention to it, and of course , I write for those who are very aware of GOD's word. For that large number of people who are not aware spiritually, I must endeavor to explain some basic Revelation and end time terminology. And for the public that I hope will read this, I endeavor to make it plain - not dumb it down, but make it plain. In doing so, I hope to encourage all to read GOD's word and read it more consistently. Revelation has been a taboo to many and some have made it a hard thing to understand, but GOD says *HIS yoke is easy; HIS burden in " LIGHT!"*

ABOMINATION of DESOLATION:
When the anti-christ sits down in the rebuilt Jewish Temple and declares himself to be God, the great tribulation of 42 months will then begin. At the occurrence of this event, the Jews living in Israel{ genuine Jews } are commanded to flee into the wilderness. All tribulation saints will know, from that day on, they must now wait 1260 days before the Lord returns. **(Dan 9:27) ,(Mat 24:15-19)**

Apocalypse:
"Apocalypse" actually means "lifting of the veil" or "revelation." The term is commonly used in the context of the end of the world. It is also used in relation to the book of Revelation or "The Apocalypse of John" which is full of visions and symbols that seem too daunting and intimidating for many. The intent of this writing is to make Revelations practical and understandable. In reality, Revelation is far less figurative and far more applicable and practical than many believe it to be. And when explained and analyzed in the light of current political realities and world events, the Apocalypse and Revelations are clear to comprehend and

crucial in understanding the world we live in. The world that is rapidly approaching its spiritual climax!

THE APOSTACY

In the end times, the Bible predicts a great falling away or departure from the faith. Because we have experienced a number of generations where people have rebelled against God, the one that occurs leading up to the tribulation will likely surpass prior apostasies. The Greek word apostasy was originally used to describe a revolt staged by a military commander. **(2 Thes 2:3), (Mat 24:11-13)**

Armageddon

Armageddon: From Hebrew -*Har Megido* (הר מגידו), "Mountain of Megiddo" in Israel is the site of the final battle between God and Satan. Satan will operate through the person known as the "Beast" or the Antichrist, written about in the Book of Revelation and in the New Testament. Moreover, it can also refer to the apocalyptic catastrophes

Pre-Tribulation and Tribulation

Jesus will remove His faithful Church sometime prior to these 1260 days of great tribulation and great deception or strong delusion.

RAPTURE

The righteous are gathered together to meet the Lord in the air, commonly called the Rapture, described in **1 Thessalonians 4:17**: *"Then we which are alive and remain shall be caught up together with them in the clouds, to meet the Lord in the air: and so shall we ever be with the Lord."* Revelation 3:10 indicates that, as believers patiently endure tribulation, they will be kept from temptation: *"Because thou hast kept the word of my patience, I also will keep thee from the hour of temptation, which shall come upon all the world, to try them that dwell upon the earth. Behold, I come quickly: hold that fast which thou hast, that no man take thy crown."*

The Second Coming

The second coming of YESHUA Christ{ Jesus} is the earnest expectation of believers that GOD is in control of all things, and is faithful to the promises and prophecies in HIS Word. In HIS first coming, YESHUA came to earth as a baby in a manger in Bethlehem, just as prophesied. HE fulfilled many of the prophecies of the Messiah during birth, life, ministry, death, and resurrection. However, there are some prophecies regarding the Messiah that YESHUA has not yet fulfilled. The second coming of Christ will be the return of Christ to fulfill these remaining prophecies. In the first coming YESHUA, was the suffering servant. In the second coming, HE will be the conquering King. In the first coming YESHUA, arrived in the most humble of circumstances. In the second coming, heads will roll and El SHADA will arrive with the armies of heaven at HIS side!

THE WRATH OF GOD:
The Wrath of God is poured out on man at the midpoint of the tribulation. The people of earth will come under God's wrath because they refuse to turn from their wicked ways. Those that receive the Antichrist Mark will not only come under God's wrath, but will be lost forever. **(1 Thes 1:10), (1 Thes 5:9) , (Rev 14:9-11)**

Tribulation

A period described in Revelations in horrific detail of the terrible pestilences, plagues & nightmarish monsters that GOD lets loose to tribulate the anti-christ forces, who are trying to wipe out all who refuse to take the mark of the beat. It will occur after the rapture. The Bible spells it out in years, months & days exactly how long this period of Great Tribulation will be...3-1/2 years, or 42 months, or 1260 days
{ **Rev. 12:6,4** }

10 Nation Confederation - Toes; Horns; Kings:
Out of the area that once was the Roman Empire, ten leaders will arise. The only purpose these 10 leaders will have is to give their power to the anti-christ.

70 YEARS of the MILLENNIUM
The world will return to a barbaric state with only a few men left over the entirety of the earth, and the wide devastation will last for 70 years **{Isaiah23:17,18}**. Thus, the first 70 years of the Millennium (after Christ comes back to earth with his judgments) will witness the earth in a very devastated state. All civilization as we know it today (or as we have known it for the past 4000 years)

will come to a sudden halt. The first 70 years of the Millennium (while the resurrected saints of God are in heaven learning how to adapt to their new spiritual bodies and the new spiritual environment that they find themselves a part of will witness a time when the few humans are left on earth

666 Mark of the Beast and End Time Nations:
Radio-Frequency Identification Transponders," and sub dermal implants may soon be used to implement a national ID in America, the forerunner of the Mark of the Beast of Revelation 13:16, without which, no one will be able to buy or sell: *"And he causeth all, both small and great, rich and poor, free and bond, to receive a mark in their right hand, or in their foreheads..."*
(Dan 7:20), {Rev 17:12), {Rev 17:17)

A CONSCIOUS READING LIST

The Bible says that we should watch and pray. No doubt those who see themselves as good Christians do pray and read GOD's word daily. But are we really following GOD's word if all we read is the Bible. The Bible says that with knowledge, we must also get understanding. ***An understanding of the WORD should behoove us to seek knowledge wherever and whenever we can from as many sources as we can.*** With this in mind , I suggest to you that many who are consistently in the Bible are not consistently into other readings that would not only help in the understanding of the Bible , but will also help give clarity and understanding to the current realities of these end time days. To watch means to be aware of the world around us! <u>Too many ministers and church goers are so politically naïve and do not know satan their adversary and how that adversary operates within governments and earthly events</u>. We offer this small reading list. " For we must be spiritually and politically conscious." This also is the job of the ***LIVING EPISTLE !*** Along with those works already mentioned, we offer those below.

Dr. Kwame Ture(Stokely Carmichael)
<u>Black Power; Stokely Speaks</u>
Kwame Nkrumah <u>Consciencism</u>

SOON AND VERY SOON

Sekou Toure <u>Revolution and Religion, Africa On The Move</u>
Amilcar Cabral <u>Return To the Source</u>
Franz Fanon <u>The Wretched of the Earth</u>
Felix Green <u>The Enemy, What Every American Should Know About American Imperialism</u>
Peter Abrams <u>The Mind of Africa</u>
W.E.B. Du Bois <u>The World and Africa</u>
Cheikh Anta Diop <u>Pre Colonial Black Africa</u>
Chancellor Williams <u>The Destruction of Black Civilization</u>
George GM James <u>Stolen Legacy</u>
Josef Ben-Jochannan <u>Africa The Origin Of Major Western Religions</u>
John Jackson <u>Introduction To African Civilization</u>

SOON AND VERY SOON

For comments and criticisms of this work, please contact:

gideonodinga@gmail.com

OTHER BOOKS AND
WRITINGS BY
Elder Gideon Odinga Mukhtar

1/ *Obama Drama: A Strategy of Neo-Liberal Deception*; Second Edition

2/ *Chickens Come Home to Roost: A Critical Analysis of American Capitalism in Crisis*

Elder Gideon is also editor of a *" FREE "* on line quarterly journal for political activist called *the Revolutionary Theory and Action Collective Journal.* To receive e journal free, send request to
gideonodinga@gmail.com

229